MARKETING

An analytical and evaluative approach to business studies

Ian Swift

Hodder & Stoughton
A MEMBER OF THE HODDER HEADLINE GROUP

Orders: please contact Bookpoint Ltd, 78 Milton Park, Abingdon, Oxon OX14 4TD. Telephone: (44) 01235 827720, Fax: (44) 01235 400454. Lines are open from 9.00 – 6.00, Monday to Saturday, with a 24 hour message answering service. Email address: orders@bookpoint.co.uk

A catalogue record for this title is available from The British Library

ISBN 0 340 75835X

First published 2000
Impression number   10 9 8 7 6 5 4 3 2
Year   2005 2004 2003 2002 2001 2000

Cover illustration by Jon H. Hamilton
Typeset by Fakenham Photosetting Ltd, Fakenham, Norfolk
Printed in Great Britain for Hodder & Stoughton Educational, a division of Hodder Headline Plc, 338 Euston Road, London NW1 3BH by JW Arrowsmith, Bristol.

Acknowledgements

I would like to dedicate this book to my wife Dawn, particularly for her patience and support during its writing, and our two sons Gary and Peter. As this is my first solo book, I would also like to take the opportunity to thank all those people who have aided my development as a teacher, examiner and writer of A Level Business Studies material.

As a teacher:
Brian Yeomans of the then Trent Polytechnic – especially for the cricketing metaphors.
Chris Dodd at Lytham St Annes High School – who taught me more about teaching, through his example, than even he realises.
Ian Haselden at Cardinal Newman College – for having faith in me and giving me room to develop.

As an examiner:
David Anderson and Peter Evans as team leaders, for early encouragement.
David Lines and Ian Marcousé as Chief Examiners, for setting the standards.
Clare Wilson and Sarah Freemantle for unstinting support and football matches at the AEB.

As a writer:
Ian Marcousé for asking in the first instance and then coming back for more.
Clare Smith, formerly at Hodder and Stoughton, for talking me into this in the first place.
Melanie Hall at Hodder for the required pushing.
Andrew Gillespie for setting the template.

The author and publisher would like to thank the following for permission to reproduce copyright material:

'New Earnings Survey', Office for National Statistics, © Crown Copyright 1999, p. 61; *Financial Times*, pp. 58, 97; Mintel International Group Ltd., pp. 61, 97.

Every effort has been made to trace copyright holders but this has not always been possible in all cases; any omissions brought to our attention will be corrected in future printings.

If you have any comments on this book or suggestions for future editions, the Series Editor would be pleased to hear from you on: **gillsp@hotmail.com**

General introduction

Using this series

This series of six books is designed specifically to develop the higher levels of skill needed for exam success and, at the same time, to provide you with a critical and detailed insight into the subject as a whole. The books are written by a team of highly experienced examiners and authors to provide you with the information and approach to achieve the best results. Whereas a traditional textbook tends to provide an explanation of topics, this series concentrates on developing ideas in a more analytical manner. When considering a topic such as marketing planning, for example, the book will focus on issues such as:

■ The value of marketing planning

■ The influences on marketing planning

■ The limitations of the planning process.

The whole approach of the series is intended to develop a questioning and evaluative understanding of business issues. The emphasis is on why certain factors are important, rather than merely describing what they are. Reading these books will provide you with new insights into topics and help you to develop a critical view of the issues involved in the different areas of the subject.

Using this book

This particular book critically examines the marketing of businesses and products. It covers the following areas:

■ an introduction to marketing

■ marketing strategies

■ marketing planning

■ marketing research

■ marketing audit

■ the marketing mix.

Throughout the text we provide up-to-date examples of business behaviour in the form of **fact files** and **numerical investigations**. There are also numerous **progress checks** in each chapter to help you to review your understanding of the topics you have covered so far. Each chapter includes sample exam questions, students' answers (including marks awarded and marker's comments) and advice on how to answer specific types of question in the exam. Answers to the end of section questions can be found in the Teacher's Handbook which accompanies the series. Chapter 8 is designed to help you interpret and analyse numerical data from this syllabus area.

Chapter 9 provides information on how the business concepts covered in the book are usually assessed in examinations and focuses on the key underlying issues in each topic; this will be invaluable when it comes to preparing for your exams.

Chapter 7 focuses on the most recent issues in this area of the syllabus to make sure you are completely up-to-date in your understanding and to provide you with the latest ideas to include in your answers.

Not only will this book provide you with a thorough understanding of the significance of marketing, it will also help you develop the approach you need to achieve top grades. It is an invaluable resource for students who want to achieve exam success.

The 'levels of response' approach to marking

In AS and A Level Business Studies candidates are assessed by their ability to demonstrate certain key skills. A student's final grade will depend on the extent to which he or she has shown the ability to analyse points, structure their ideas and come to a reasoned conclusion. An A grade candidate is someone who demonstrates these skills consistently, whereas a C grade candidate shows them intermittently. To do well at AS and A level, students not only have to know the issues involved in each topic area, they also have to be able to develop their ideas. It is very important, therefore, that candidates provide some depth to their answers, rather than leaving many ideas undeveloped. In most cases students do better by analysing a few key points in their answers, rather than by listing many different ideas. Unfortunately, many students find it difficult to expand on their initial points; although they often demonstrate a good knowledge of the issues involved, they do not necessarily find it easy to explore these ideas further. The aim of this series of books is specifically to help you develop your ideas in more depth, which will enable you to do better in the exam.

The basic approach to assessment at AS and A Level is the same for all the examination boards and is known as 'levels of response' marking. In its simplest form this means that the mark you get depends on the skill you have demonstrated. The higher the skill shown in your answer the higher your final mark.

There are four main levels of skill assessed at A Level. These are:

- synthesis and evaluation   (the highest level skill)
- analysis
- explanation and application
- identification   (the lowest level)

As you can see the 'identification' of relevant factors is the lowest level skill. This means that listing ideas will not in itself achieve a high grade. What is important is that you explain these points (i.e. show what they mean) analyse them (i.e. show why they are significant) and evaluate them (i.e. weigh up their relative importance).

In a typical question worth 9 marks the mark scheme may look something like this:

- Candidate *evaluates* relevant factors   9–7 marks
- Candidate *analyses* relevant factors   6–5 marks
- Candidate *explains* or applies relevant factors   4–3 marks
- Candidate *identifies* relevant factors   2–1 marks

As you can see, a candidate who simply identifies factors can only achieve a maximum score of 2 out of 9. Regardless of how many different points he or she makes, if all the student has done is to list ideas they cannot get more than 2 marks in total. To move up the levels and gain more marks candidates need to demonstrate the higher level skills. Unfortunately, most textbooks spend so much time explaining ideas that they cannot do much to help develop the ability to analyse and evaluate. This series focuses throughout on these higher level skills to help you move up the levels of response in the exam and maximise your grade.

Imagine you were faced with a question which asked you to 'Discuss the factors which might influence a firm's marketing strategy.' A good answer would identify a few relevant factors, explain what is meant by them, develop their impact and then discuss their importance. For example:

'A firm's marketing strategy will depend on its marketing objectives, the market opportunities and its own marketing strengths. The strategy will be strongly influenced by the objectives – a desire to increase sales within the existing market may make the firm focus on new segments or try to increase usage rates. If, however, the objective is to stabilise overall sales, the firm might seek to diversify into new markets. Any strategy should be firmly based on the firm's strengths (according to an asset-led marketing approach). For example, Virgin might build its strategy on its brand name, Microsoft might exploit its technical expertise, Apple and 3M might build on their ability to innovate, W.H. Smith might try to use its store network. A strategy which is not related to a firm's skills and assets is likely to be risky; the firm might be overstretched or exposed. The strategy must also relate to the external environment – attempts to expand in declining markets, the launch of income elastic consumer goods in a recession or an export push with a strong pound are not likely to be successful.'

This is a strong answer which takes a couple of points and develops them in some depth. For comparison, consider this answer:

Marketing strategy depends on 'assets, opportunities, marketing skills, the competition and the marketing budget. The nature of the market is also important and so are the firm's objectives.' This answer has many ideas but all of them are left undeveloped and so it is a much weaker answer.

More recent mark schemes adopt a slightly different approach in which content, application, analysis and evaluation are each given a mark, as in Table 1.1. As you can see in this case (which is the mark scheme for an essay) you can gain up to 8 marks for content, 8 marks for application, 8 for analysis and 16 for evaluation.

Within each category the levels approach is used so that strong evaluation can be awarded up to 16 marks, whereas more limited evaluation may only get 2 or 3 marks. The basic principles of this scheme are similar to the original levels of response model; certainly the message to candidates is clear: the higher marks require analysis and evaluation; the best marks require good analysis and evaluation! A content laden answer would only get a maximum of 8 marks.

SKILL	CONTENT	APPLICATION	ANALYSIS	EVALUATION
Maximum number of marks	8 marks	8 marks	8 marks	16 marks
Level of response	8–5 marks Three or more relevant factors identified	8–6 marks Full explanation of factors	8–6 marks Full analysis using theory appropriately and accurately	16–11 marks Mature judgement shown in arguments and conclusions
	4–3 marks Two relevant factors identified	5–3 marks Some explanation of two or more factors	5–3 marks Analysis with some use of relevant theory	10–5 marks Judgement shown in arguments and/or conclusions
	2–1 marks One relevant factor identified	2–1 marks Some explanation of one factor	2–1 marks Limited analysis of question	4–1 marks Some judgement shown in text or conclusions
	0 marks No knowledge shown	0 marks No application or explanation	0 marks No analysis present	0 marks No judgement shown

Table 1.1 Example mark scheme

The key to success in examinations is to consistently demonstrate the ability to analyse and evaluate – this involves exploring a few of the points you have made. All of the books in this series take an approach which should develop your critical ability and make it easier for you to discuss your ideas in more depth.

The higher level skills

What is analysis?

To analyse a point you need to show why it *matters*. Why is it relevant to the question? Why is it important? Having made a point and explained what it actually means, you need to discuss its significance either by examining what caused it or by exploring its effect on the business.

Question: *Analyse the possible value of market research for a firm.*

Answer: Market research enables a firm to make better decisions (*point made*) because it provides managers with information. This means they do not have to rely so much on hunches (*explanation*). Therefore, their decisions are likely to be less risky, because they should have some basis in fact (although research cannot guarantee success) (*analysis*).

The answer above provides a logical chain of thought: market research provides information on which to base decisions, thereby reducing the element of risk. A second example is given below.

Question: *Analyse the factors which might influence the size of a firm's marketing budget.*

Answer: The budget may depend on the marketing plan (*point made*): the nature of the plan will determine what resources are needed to implement it successfully (*explanation*). The launch of a new product nationally, for example, is likely to require a bigger budget than a specific local advertising campaign. The amount spent will also depend on the expected returns because if the returns are low the amount spent is also likely to be lower (*analysis*).

Again the thought process is logical. If the firm has an ambitious plan involving high expected returns this is likely to involve a relatively high marketing budget.

What is synthesis?

Synthesis occurs when an answer is *structured effectively*. Essentially, it involves writing well organised answers rather than leaving it up to the reader to make sense of the argument. In a 'discussion' question this means putting an argument for a case, an argument against and then a conclusion.

Synthesis tends to come from planning your answer, rather than starting writing immediately. Whenever you face a question, try to sort out what you want each paragraph to say before you begin to write the answer out in full. This should lead to a better organised response. A final paragraph to bring together the arguments is also recommended.

What is evaluation?

Evaluation is the highest skill and involves demonstrating some form of *judgement*. Once you have developed various points you have to show which one or ones are most important or under what circumstances these issues are most likely to be significant. Evaluation involves some reflection on the arguments for and against and some thought about which aspects are most important.

This often involves standing back from your argument to decide what would make your ideas more or less relevant. Ask yourself under what circumstances would one course of action be chosen rather than another. This process is illustrated below.

Question: *Discuss the possible benefits of marketing planning.*

Answer: Marketing planning involves an assessment of the future (*point made*) because a plan must be based on some forecast of the position of the market, customer needs and requirements and competitors' offerings (*explanation*).

This may mean that the firm is better prepared for market conditions and that its response is an integrated and well co-ordinated one. By looking ahead and developing a view of the market, managers are more likely to consider the implications of this for the firm in terms of production, finance, and people. Without any form of planning, managers may be taken by surprise and find themselves reacting to events, rather than anticipating (or even determining) them (*analysis*).

However, the value of planning depends on the accuracy of the plan itself and its flexibility. If the plan is inappropriate or based on a set of assumptions which are no longer relevant, then the marketing is unlikely to be successful. It may even be harmful if employees focus on the plan rather than using their initiative to react to events (*evaluation*).

To evaluate your arguments you need to think carefully about whether the points you have made earlier in your answer are *always* true. What makes them more or less true? What makes the impact more or less severe? To what extent can the firm avoid or exploit the situation you have described? To evaluate effectively you have to imagine different organisations and think about what factors would influence them to act in one way or another. What would make the impact of change greater or smaller? Evaluation, therefore, requires a broad appreciation of the factors which influence a firm's decisions and an awareness of the variety of organisations present in the business world.

We hope you find these books useful. They are designed to be very different from typical textbooks in that they will help you use ideas and think about their importance. At the same time, these books will provide you with new ideas about topics and, we hope, will convey some of the passion and enthusiasm we have for such a fascinating subject.

Summary chart

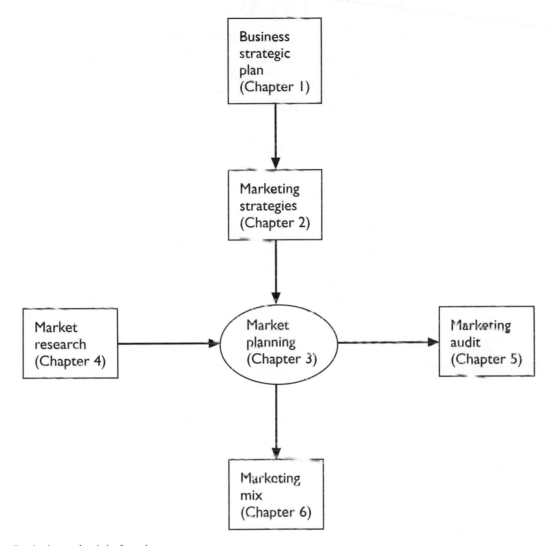

How the elements of marketing fit together

Overview

Introduction

Marketing is a critical business activity which links an organisation to its customers. Effective marketing enables a firm to identify and even anticipate customer needs and wants and to provide a product or service which not only satisfies customers but delights them. At the same time, effective marketing ensures that the firm itself benefits from the exchange process. Marketing is not simply about making customers happy – it is about meeting the organisation's own objectives as well. In the case of private sector organisations, this usually means that the firm wants to make a profit from each transaction; however, the marketing process is applicable to *all* organisations, not just profit-making ones. Political parties, religious groups, sports clubs and government services all use marketing to achieve their own goals.

FACT FILE

In the late 1990s, the Conservative Party launched a 'Listening to Britain' campaign. After its crushing defeat in the 1997 General Election by the Labour Party, the Conservative Party was eager to find out what it had done wrong! Much of the success of the Labour Party under Tony Blair was said to be due to its ability to target the uncertain voter and, after successful market research, offer them the policies they wanted.

The Church of England also actively engaged in marketing in the 1990s to try and increase the number of people attending Church. The marketing included some fairly extensive and thought provoking advertising campaigns.

What is marketing?

Perhaps because marketing activities are so visible to all of us, in the form of promotional campaigns, market research and new product development, there is a tendency to assume that we all understand it intuitively. Nearly all of us know someone involved in marketing and we have some sense that it involves sales, promotions and advertising. However, the 'true' nature of marketing and its significance is not so well known. People often have a very limited view of marketing activities and do not always appreciate the way in which, within successful organisations, the philosophy of marketing is part of every aspect of the business.

Some of the common (and, in many cases, inappropriate and limiting) assumptions consumers hold about marketing are that:

- '*Marketing is advertising.*' Certainly, advertising is *one* aspect of marketing, and it is often a highly visible activity. Wherever you look, whether at television, on the high street, in shops, newspapers and magazines, you will see many examples of advertising. Marketing, though, is a lot more than just advertising. The tasks undertaken by the marketing function in a business include: decisions about product features, price, packaging, distribution and positioning.

- '*Marketing is selling.*' To a degree, this view is more accurate. One of the ultimate aims of marketing is to *increase sales* of the company's products. However, the word 'selling' is a bit simplistic. Marketing tries to answer these questions: Who are we selling to? What do they want to be sold? How do we know what they want? Who else is trying to sell them something similar? The actions of customers and competitors, as well as those of the business, must be considered if the marketing function is to be successful.

■ *'Marketing is getting people to buy products they don't really want.'* Who needs an electric toothbrush? Furry dice for the car? Fridge magnets in the shape of fruit? Think of the things you have bought recently. Why did you buy them? There is a very fine line between buying something because it fulfils a need and buying something because of the **image** that it portrays. Of course, images are created by clever marketing. As we shall see later, part of marketing is to *create* a need in consumers' minds. However, marketers can not do this from scratch. At best, they can develop ideas that people already have.

PROGRESS CHECK

Questions

1 Take one of the common assumptions described above. List as many arguments for and against the viewpoint as you can. Then decide from your points which 'side' has the stronger argument.
2 If advertising encourages consumers to buy products they otherwise wouldn't, do you think advertising is ethical?

Of course, there is an element of truth to each of the above ideas. However, the *degree* to which they are true can be debated endlessly.

Defining marketing

Components of a definition

There are many different definitions that exist, but the most widely accepted ones are likely to contain the following factors:

■ *An outward-looking perspective*: marketing takes account of the requirements of the marketplace. What needs do consumers have that are not currently being fulfilled? What are competitors doing? What are consumers thinking? Marketing focuses very clearly on consumers' wants and needs. Everything that everyone does within the organisation has to be considered in terms of its likely impact on customer satisfaction.

■ *A consistent and integrated approach*: for example, ensuring that the price to be charged suits the product, its image and the outlet being used. Any discrepancy between these elements may confuse consumers and prevent them from making a purchase.

■ *A commitment to the goals of the business*: marketing is only one function within the whole business. It is important that it works with all the other functions to achieve the objectives of the business. Marketing should be strategic – it is vital to think about how it can contribute to the long-run success of the firm. Whilst the price of a particular product or the colour of its packaging may be important in the short term, in the long run what really matters is whether the firm is in the right market at all. If the market is declining it does not matter what the price is.

FACT FILE

When Daewoo entered the UK car market in 1995 it had many disadvantages, such as the lack of a track record and no brand recognition. However, it was able to successfully penetrate the market through a clear customer focus based on four propositions:

1 direct dealing to keep prices down
2 absence of hassle (such as no haggling over prices)
3 full 3 year warranties to give peace of mind
4 free collection, delivery and courtesy cars.

■ *A mutually beneficial exchange process*: marketing is a two-way process in which both sides benefit; the consumer benefits from the product or service, whilst the firm benefits from the revenue it receives.

> **Marketing is not just about making the customer happy.**

'Offensive marketing'

One of the best definitions of marketing is provided by Hugh Davidson in his excellent book, *Even More Offensive Marketing*. 'Offensive marketing involves every employee in building superior customer value very efficiently for above average profits.'

There are some very important points to note in this definition. Firstly, that marketing needs to be offensive rather than passive; firms must be proactive rather than wait for things to happen. Secondly, marketing involves everyone in the organisation, not just marketing specialists. Thirdly, Davidson stresses the need to build *superior* value, not just good value – 'a business has to offer something that is not only good in its own right, but better than the competitors'. Davidson's definition also focuses on the financial side of marketing; firms must ensure their marketing is efficient and generates, not just adequate profits, but above average profits. Many people seem to forget that marketing involves costs and that firms want profits as a result. Marketing success should be judged in these terms.

The changing face of marketing

There is a lot of evidence to suggest that the role of marketing within business is changing as the nature of business itself changes. In the early part of the twentieth century, as mass production became the norm, firms produced goods with, apparently, little regard for the wants of consumers. Henry Ford famously suggested that customers could buy their cars in any colour they wanted as long as it was black. This is often quoted as proof that firms were more product orientated than consumer orientated. As the century progressed, two things changed that forced firms to take more account of their customers. Firstly, the number of firms increased and businesses grew larger, making many markets more competitive. Businesses soon found that the most effective way to keep ahead of competitors was to provide consumers with what they wanted, rather than expecting them to buy whatever the business choose to produce. Secondly, industrial growth also led consumers to become better off. Having greater spending power inevitably gives consumers a greater say in their spending habits. They were willing to spend more if it meant that they were going to receive a product that suited their needs better.

Internal marketing

Competition and income together forced firms to become aware of the needs of consumers, and the second half of the twentieth century has been characterised by the idea of **consumer sovereignty**. There are also signs that the move towards consumer orientation, both inside and outside businesses, is continuing as the twenty-first century starts. Consider, for example, the ideas of **cell production**. This is a way of organising a production line so that it is split up into several self-contained units, each producing a significant part of a finished article. An underlying principle of this system is to treat other cells further down the production line as customers of 'your' cell. The basic marketing questions (such as: How many products do they want? When do they want them? What standard is required of the work?) apply just as much to such 'internal' customers as they do to 'external' customers.

Total Quality Management

Another concept that is being widely adopted is **Total Quality Management**. In essence, this means making sure that a culture of quality is adopted by everyone who works in the business. From a marketing perspective, customers expect products that work properly and do the task for which they were bought. Since everyone in the business is involved in ensuring the quality of the product, it follows that everyone is involved in the fundamental marketing task of meeting the needs of customers. Marketing can, therefore, be said to involve everyone in the business, whatever their status or official role.

The widely respected management writer, Peter Drucker, has suggested that the role of marketing is of such great importance to a business that it extends beyond any and all of the tasks normally associated with it. He feels that marketing is the 'whole business' as seen from the 'customers' point of view'. Everything a business does, in his opinion, is part of marketing. Production, personnel and even accounting all contribute to fulfilling the needs of consumers, and so they are a part of the marketing of the business. In this sense, everyone in the business is involved in marketing.

Marketing in different firms

Different firms have different approaches to running all aspects of their business. The ideas that underpin the marketing role, therefore, vary from firm to firm. In broad terms, there are three possible approaches that firms could adopt, although in reality it is very difficult to find clear cut examples of any of them. The actual situation, as with many theoretical ideas in business, will be a mixture, drawing on all three approaches, varying from one circumstance to another and changing over time.

The three approaches can be thought of as a continuum, as shown in figure 1.1. At one extreme, firms tend to consider their strengths and assets when making marketing decisions (product orientation), whilst at the other extreme the customer rules in every case. The central ground is taken by firms which attempt to match the strengths of the company with the needs of the customer (asset-led). Each of these ideas will be considered in more detail below.

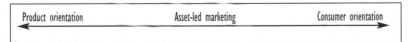

| Product orientation | Asset-led marketing | Consumer orientation |

Figure 1.1 A continuum of marketing ideas

KEY TERM

Consumer sovereignty
is the idea that the decision to buy a product is determined by the consumers' buying habits alone.

FACT FILE

At the turn of the millennium, one of the more intriguing marketing predictions came from Gregory Carpenter, an American professor of marketing, who believed that the challenge of the twenty-first century for marketers would be to move from consumer orientation — giving customers what they want — to actually driving the market so that customers want the products in which your company has a competitive advantage.

Product orientation

In its most extreme version, firms which adopt a product orientation will be very inward looking. They will consider their own strengths and ideas, and take little, if any, heed of the demands being made in the marketplace. There are rare circumstances in which such an approach could be successful: the marketplace would need to be very *static* with *few competitors*. The firm would not be aware of changes in the market, such as new ideas from competitors, or changes in taste and fashion. Product-orientated firms need a *loyal consumer base* so that products continue to be sold in the absence of significant marketing activities. Taking these three characteristics together, it is obvious that product-orientated firms are unlikely to survive for long as mass producers of fast-moving consumer goods. However, they may have a chance of survival in niche markets and as producers of industrial products. For example, Morgan Cars appears to be a firm which pays little attention to the advances being made in motor car technology or the demands for comfort and economy made by customers on mass produced vehicles. The car is never advertised and models are updated infrequently. Nevertheless, the demand for Morgan cars outstrips the rate at which the firm can produce them. Despite the possibility of increased sales, though, the firm remains true to its own tried and trusted methods of production and makes little effort to update its production methods.

Market orientation

Market orientation is, in many ways, the exact opposite of product orientation. Market research results are closely analysed in order to determine the requirements of the consumer. When a **market opportunity** is identified, the firm goes all out to meet that need. When such a policy is successful, the firm will always be one step ahead of its competitors. However, if other firms are trying to follow similar strategies, any advantage one firm gains by being first into the market with a new development will soon disappear as competitors catch up or bring out refinements of the original idea. The advantage of being market orientated is clear – since the firm is always meeting the needs of the consumer, there ought to be a clear demand for their products. The disadvantages of market orientation, however, are often overlooked:

■ Marketing opportunities may be short-lived, if they arise at all.

■ A market-orientated firm places a lot of faith in market research, and as will be seen in Chapter 4, market research is not always as reliable as it seems.

■ Consumer needs are constantly changing. Any strategy which involves keeping up with these needs implies constant change on the part of the business as well. Business theory tells us that the management of change is one of the most difficult aspects of management.

■ There is a danger that firms may identify market opportunities which are viable in themselves but which do not meet with their own strengths. There are thousands of business opportunities available to organisations at any moment; firms must be careful to choose those which fit with their own abilities.

Asset-led marketing

The middle ground of the continuum of marketing ideas seeks to mix elements of both the extremes. Asset-led marketing tries to match the identified needs of the marketplace with the strengths of the business. Here the word 'assets' is taken in its widest meaning. It implies that the experience and expertise of the workforce and management, brand names and company image, as well as the tangible assets of machinery and plant are considered when the firm is looking for opportunities to develop in the marketplace. For example, a firm such as Rolls Royce might undertake research which finds that a niche exists for an economical, 'runabout' type of car which has a touch of luxury in terms of interior fittings, seating and so on. The firm, however, may decide that such a vehicle would not suit the company name and image, and that it could even bring the brand name down-market, to the detriment of their existing products. Whilst a market-orientated firm may jump at the chance of exploiting a new market niche, an asset-led firm is more likely to reject the idea and look for something which builds on the existing strengths of the firm. In theory, at least, an asset-led firm has the best of both worlds in that it takes into account the changing needs of the marketplace, whilst only pursuing ideas that exploit the existing strengths of the business.

So, why is it that not all firms follow an asset-led philosophy? The answer lies in resources and individual circumstances. Marketing information is relatively cheap and readily available; with the impact of information technology it is becoming even more so. In some firms, however, the skills needed to exploit this data may not be available.

In addition, **information overload** is a very real problem and in some firms the right information may not reach the right people at the right time. It may also be the case that, in some firms, the marketing department does not have a powerful voice at the level where business decisions are made. Traditional-style managers, perhaps with a background in production or finance, may give less weight to marketing ideas than to innovative products or products which have been found to be profitable. The change in direction implied by asset-led marketing may not be generally accepted. Market conditions may prevent asset-led marketing. A highly competitive market may force firms to abandon their traditional strengths to keep hold of their market share.

So, although asset led marketing can be considered an ideal approach for a business, its application depends to a great extent on the individual circumstances and characteristics of the business itself. Clearly firms will, at different times and in different circumstances, adopt different approaches to marketing. If a firm has time and resources on its side, it could well adopt an asset-led approach. In times of crisis with few resources and the need for a rapid response to the actions of competitors, firms might move towards one or other end of the continuum.

Adding value

Whatever approach a firm adopts for its marketing, there is one over-riding objective that must be tackled in every circumstance. This is the need to **add value**.

Adding value means being able to charge more for the output than the total cost of the related inputs. From one perspective, added value is a consequence of the production process. A carpenter takes as inputs some woods, nails and varnish, a proportion of the cost of tools and his or her own time. The final product, a television cabinet, is worth more than all these inputs put together, so clearly there has been value added to the product somewhere between the start and end of the process. The act of production – the combining of the raw materials through the skills of the worker – has been a key element in adding value. Marketing also adds value: the purchaser of the product must be *convinced* that the finished cabinet is worth more than the various elements that went into its manufacture. The finished product must have an image or meet a need so that consumers are encouraged to pay more for the product than its actual cost. This example clearly demonstrates the basic function of marketing: to provide a perceived benefit for the customer that allows the firm to charge more than the product actually cost.

Replica football shirts are another example. They have developed an image over the last decade or so that makes them valuable as fashion items and almost a necessity for anyone who actually goes and watches their favourite team playing. Although firms are secretive about their costs, it is generally assumed that a replica shirt costs in the region of £5 to £7 to manufacture, and yet the end product can be sold for up to £45. The additional cost is the price of the image of the shirt and its associated football team. In this case, the image of the product has provided a value that the customer is willing to pay for; in other cases value may be added because the producer has done the work for the consumer.

Convenience food from the freezer and fast food outlets have added value because they meet a need in today's lifestyle. Many people lead busy work and social lives and do not wish to spend their time cooking meals as a daily chore. Food companies do the work for the consumer, fulfil a need in the marketplace and so add value to the basic ingredients that they use. Without added value products are not desirable and firms will not be successful.

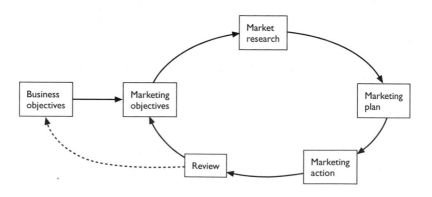

Figure 1.2 The marketing model

Adding value by marketing

In practice, the adding of value to a firm's products comes about through the application of the **marketing model** (figure 1.2). This is a framework from which the firm can determine its marketing decisions. In many ways, the framework is similar to other decision-making models in that it adopts a circular pattern, implying that marketing is a continual process that is under constant review, always adapting to changing situations and circumstances.

Although there are many different versions of the marketing model, its basic form has five stages. The starting point must be the **overall objectives** of the business. The marketing function must help the business achieve its overall aims if it is to be worthwhile.

From the objectives of the business, a broad marketing strategy can be devised. This involves setting the marketing agenda in general terms. Using this outline plan and a knowledge of the marketplace, a detailed marketing plan, setting out the actions to be taken, can be devised. Once the plan is put into practice, the results can be assessed. It can then be decided whether or not to continue with the same plan or, if need be, to change the strategy.

In many ways, the most important aspect of the whole marketing model is the 'review'. The review function implies learning from past and current experiences. Even the best plans do not work perfectly. The purpose of the review is to analyse both successes and failures. What happened that was unexpected? What lessons can be learned from the experience? By answering such questions as truthfully and as completely as possible, the firm will be better equipped to make plans for the future.

Is marketing becoming more important?

Arguably, marketing is becoming more important because of increasing levels of competition, ever faster product development, new ways of competing (e.g. via the Internet) and ever more demanding customers. Markets are fragmenting, customers expect higher standards of quality and, with more and more trade barriers coming down, competition is often global. In such circumstances the firms which best understand and work *with* their customers, the organisations which listen and react quickly and the businesses which build on their marketing assets are likely to be in a stronger position. With greater choice and greater access to information, customers are less likely to put up with second best, inadequate services or poor quality; in this sense marketing has become more important as it dictates a quality philosophy and approach which must run throughout the business. However, the marketing function must also act in co-ordination with the other elements of the organisation – marketing alone cannot determine a firm's success. Success also depends on the effective management of people and operations, and appropriate financial planning. A good understanding of customer requirements is of limited value without the ability to actually respond to it. The importance of marketing

must, therefore, be placed in context; what is important is that the firm continually strives to improve (because competitors will also be trying to improve and, if a firm stands still, it will fall behind). Improvements can only be made if the functions of the business are co-ordinated and its strategies build both on market opportunities and the firm's strengths.

The marketing department

The advantage of creating a marketing department is that it brings together specialists who can work as a team, share experiences and focus on marketing activities. The use of experts can lead to better decision-making and, as a result, more successful marketing. However, there is no absolute need for a formal marketing department and creating one does not guarantee effective marketing. As we have seen, marketing is everyone's job and, certainly in many smaller organisations, marketing activities are carried out as part of other jobs. Marketing, ultimately, is more about the way that people within the organisation think and plan, rather than a departmental title. The real question is not whether a firm has a marketing department but whether the customer plays the central role in its thinking.

Summary chart

Figure 1.3 Key elements of an introduction to marketing

Approaching exam questions: Overview

Evaluate the possible impact of inadequate marketing on a producer of fast-moving consumer goods.

(11 marks)

Questions like this set a simple trap into which many students fall. A heavy stress is placed on the importance of marketing during most business courses, so students tend to assume that the answer to the equation must be extreme. Many students would use phrases such as 'the result would be catastrophic' or 'the business will inevitably go into liquidation'. However, a good answer to such a question will achieve a *balanced* viewpoint.

To do this candidates can employ two approaches:

1 The answer ought to contain 'balanced' language. That is, instead of writing 'will inevitably lead to liquidation' phrases such as '*could* lead to liquidation' or 'will *often* cause problems for the firm' should be used instead. In this way, extreme views are toned down and a degree of careful consideration is introduced.
2 Even with an apparently one-sided question, there will still be scope for a two-sided answer. 'Inadequate marketing' implies that *some* marketing is taking place. In what ways is it inadequate? Is it under funded, or misdirected? How long has the inadequacy been present? What reasons may there be for the inadequacies? Given that there are varying degrees of inadequacy, there must be a wide range of possible outcomes.

So, whilst there may be a strong line of argument to suggest that inadequate marketing will be bad for a business, there may also be moderating factors that will reduce the negative impact. Indeed, it is possible to argue that, if the products are good enough, they don't need marketing – spending less on unneeded marketing could improve the performance of the business.

A key factor to consider here is the type of product or market identified in the question. The fast-moving consumer goods market is usually highly competitive, implying that firms have to strive for any competitive advantage that they can get. So, although in general terms and under some conditions, inadequate marketing may not cause problems for a firm, in this particular case it could be argued that the inadequacies are likely to lead to a weakened competitive position which could jeopardise the future of the business.

'Marketing acts as a "look-out" for a business.' Discuss the extent to which marketers should concentrate on what is happening outside the business.

(11 marks)

A question that requires a discussion of 'the extent to which ...' is asking for a two-sided consideration of the issue. In this case, the issue underpinning the question is asset-led marketing, where marketers try to strike a balance between the demands of the marketplace (consumer orientation) and the skills and assets of the business.

Possible lines of argument for marketers keeping a close watch on the marketplace could be:

■ the earlier changes are identified, the quicker the possible response

■ only by studying the market can opportunities and threats be identified

■ firms must respond to the demands and wants of consumers, and these can only be discovered through market research.

On the other hand, firms should also be inward-looking for these reasons:

■ if the firm knows its strengths, it can exploit them

■ by concentrating on those aspects that the firm is good at it will be in a strong competitive position

■ the firm will avoid the risks inherent in taking on projects at which it has no advantage over competitors.

A balanced conclusion would note the strengths of both sides of this argument and raise the possibility of a middle ground approach, such as asset-led marketing.

Discuss whether or not a firm should change its marketing plans every time an external factor changes.

(11 marks)

Discussion questions such as this are looking for a two-sided, balanced view of the relevant factors. Whilst there are arguments for responding to external changes, such as changes in consumer demand and the actions of competitors in order to retain a competitive advantage, it is not practical to suggest that firms change *every* time an external factor changes. Problems associated with rapid and frequent change are:

■ the difficulties of managing change

■ the problems of co-ordinating many, possibly small, changes throughout a large organisation

■ the difficulties of gathering sufficient accurate knowledge on which to base the decision to change.

If you consider the points listed, you will see that whilst the 'for' points are based on marketing theory, the 'against' issues take the debate wider and consider the whole business. Taking the wider view in this way clearly demonstrates higher level skills such as analysis and evaluation.

A conclusion could concentrate on the word 'every' in the question. Of course, businesses should change in response to changing situations, but they should only make significant changes when the time is right, instead of attempting to change the business 'every' time an external change is detected.

'Too much emphasis is placed on marketing in today's business world.' Assess this viewpoint.

(40 marks)

An assessment of a particular viewpoint should involve arguments that both support and refute the ideas being expressed. It is unlikely that any given statement is completely false or unarguably correct, so the ultimate conclusion to the essay will be that the statement is true *to an extent* or in *certain circumstances*, but that there are also strong arguments against the viewpoint. Rather than sitting on the fence, however, good essays often reach a conclusion that, on balance, in most cases the statement is likely to be true, or untrue, depending on the issues raised in the scenario itself.

In the case of this essay, support for the statement could include such factors as:

- It is no longer sufficient to have a good product – it can be outsold by the image created for an inferior product.

- Many firms spend vast amounts of money on advertising, sponsorship, etc. For some firms this is money they can ill afford and it only allows them to achieve parity with other producers.

- Marketing is not always a 'productive' way to spend a firm's limited resources.

On the other hand, the statement may not be correct because:

- If firms can not compete effectively they are less likely to thrive and even survive.

- The increasing availability of information allows better quality marketing decisions, making it a much more important tool for business success.

- Consumer orientation is vital for a firm's long-term survival, implying that the marketing function, which promotes consumer orientation, is central to a firm's success or failure.

On balance, though, it may be said that whilst marketing is likely to be important to a business, it is only one aspect of the full range of functions carried out by the business, each of which ought to be done well if the business is to achieve its overall aims and objectives.

Student answers

Assess the ways in which marketing may add value to a firm's products.

(11 marks)

Student answer

Adding value to a product is what allows a firm to charge more for the goods or service than it actually cost, so making a profit for the firm.

The marketing department in a business can add value by promoting an image of the product in the minds of customers that makes it seem like the product is actually worth more. Fashionable clothes, for example, cost as much to make as any other set of clothes but can be sold for a lot more in the shops. This is because marketing has made people think that it is fashionable to wear such items, so people will pay more for them.

Marker's comments

This answer is clearly based on an understanding of both the concept of adding value and the role of marketing in promoting an image of a product. However, the points made are easily lost amongst the poor quality of language, and the answer as a whole comes across as being repetitive and one dimensional.

It is noticeable that there is no attempt at evaluation in terms of the importance of marketing to the creation of added value or a wider consideration of other factors that can create it. Therefore, there are no marks for evaluation.

Mark: Content 2/2, Application & Analysis 3/6, Evaluation 0/3. Total = 5

Analyse why some firms do not adopt an asset-led strategy to marketing.

(9 marks)

Student answer

There are many reasons why firms do not adopt an asset-led marketing strategy.

1 They may have no knowledge of what is meant by the term 'asset-led' marketing. If the managers have all been appointed on the basis of experience and not qualification they may never have studied business and so will make decisions on the basis of experience. A firm that has always been product orientated may always stay that way unless someone is appointed who knows about such things as asset-led marketing.

2 The firm's strengths may lie in its ability to respond quickly to changing conditions in the market place. If so, it is reacting to needs from outside the firm and so is consumer orientated. By giving the customers what

they want, the firm may need to go beyond its own specialist area and resources, again preventing an asset-led approach.

Overall, not all firms are asset led or need to be. It is just one way a firm can achieve success; not being asset led doesn't mean a firm will always fail.

Marker's comments

This answer has identified two valid points relating to reasons why firms may not be asset led. Both points are developed in an appropriate way, and the points being made are always directed back to the question set.

As a general rule, it is not a good idea to write in numbered sections – they tend to reduce the scope for developing an idea or creating flow. In this case, however, there is a basic development of each point made.

Mark: Content 2/2, Application 3/4, Analysis 2/3. Total = 7

Discuss whether market orientation is essential to business success.

(11 marks)

Student answer

There are many people who would argue that market orientation is essential for business success. Market orientation aims to put the consumer at the centre of everything that the business does. It is only by taking account of what the customer wants that a business can stay in business. If the business produces something that customers do not want, the product will not sell and the business could fail.

However the firm could produce a product and then persuade the public that they actually want it. If the firm can create a positive image for a product by linking it to a superstar or something fashionable, it may make consumers use the product.

So, although it is usually the case that a firm that is not consumer orientated will not be successful, there will be times when the opposite is true.

Marker's comments

This answer adopts a sensible structure in that it considers both sides of the argument in turn before attempting to reach a conclusion. The points are fair, and the candidate seems to have a reasonable idea about the basic debate.

It is unfortunate, however, that the points are poorly expressed and that there is no great depth to the analysis of the points made. The attempted evaluation is very basic and merely serves to repeat points that have been made previously without adding to the scope of the answer. As such it is not rewarded – the evaluation should consider when market orientation is and when it is not essential.

Mark Content 2/4, Application & Analysis 3/6, Evaluation 0/3. Total = 5

Assess the usefulness of the marketing model to a manager.

(11 marks)

Student answer

The marketing model is a process by which marketing decisions can be made, reviewed and amended. It is an attempt to give marketing decisions a scientific basis, so that a firm can have confidence that the decisions being made are the appropriate ones. Without a model such as this, marketing decisions could become little more than guesses as to what will sell at what prices and to which market segment.

There may be times when a marketing model is not wholly appropriate. If a quick decision is needed, the full marketing model may take too long to follow through, and so a decision may be made on the basis of past experience or readily available data. There is also scope for some intuition, as shown by the launch of the Walkman by Sony – the firm went against the findings of marketing research.

The marketing model, then, is a fair basis on which to make most decisions, but will not always be appropriate. It may be best to blend the scientific approach with some degree of individuality and initiative.

Marker's comments

This is clearly quite a high quality answer. The candidate has a good knowledge of the marketing model and its usefulness to a business. There is a solid body of content and each point is developed in the context of the question. There are aspects of evaluation throughout the answer, and the concluding comments round off the answer to good effect.

Mark Content 2/2, Application & Analysis 6/6, Evaluation 1/3. Total = 9

End of section questions

1 Analyse the possible impact for a firm of a change from product orientation to market orientation.

(9 marks)

2 Examine the reasons why a firm may not wish to outsource its marketing function.

(9 marks)

3 Examine the factors that might influence a firm's marketing plan.

(9 marks)

4 In what ways could asset-led marketing contribute to the success of a business?

(9 marks)

5 Why must a marketing model be cyclical in nature?

(9 marks)

6 Examine the ways in which marketing can contribute to achieving the objectives of a business.

(9 marks)

7 Discuss the ways in which marketing can 'add value' to a product.

(11 marks)

8 Examine the circumstances in which product orientation may be a viable strategy.

(9 marks)

9 Analyse the impact competitors may have on a firm's marketing plans.

(9 marks)

10 Evaluate the usefulness of using asset-led marketing for a business.

(11 marks)

Essays

1 Evaluate the usefulness of the marketing model to a newly formed small firm.

(40 marks)

2 Many public companies are accused of adopting short-term plans for short-term profits. Assess the impact this may have on the marketing function.

(40 marks)

3 If part of the task of marketing is to persuade consumers to buy products they otherwise wouldn't buy, can the marketing function ever be said to be ethical?

(40 marks)

4 To what extent does effective marketing determine a firm's success?

(40 marks)

5 Discuss the main effects that recent improvements in IT may have on marketing.

(40 marks)

Marketing strategies

Introduction

Strategy is one of the most widely used words in business. Unfortunately, it is also one of the most widely misused words as well. The term 'strategy' is often used to mean exactly the same as 'plan', 'tactics' or 'ideas', yet each of these has a different, specific meaning in the business context. Any discussion of marketing strategy, therefore, should begin with a careful consideration of the meaning of the term. Although the definitions given in different text books and journals vary, they tend to contain similar key features, suggesting that a marketing strategy is **forward-looking**, **long-term**, carefully **considered** and **relevant** to the circumstances of the specific business. This clearly differentiates a strategy from a short-term tactic; from an instant reaction to changing circumstances.

The importance of strategy

Marketing strategies can take many forms, even within the same business. At any one time, a firm could be following different marketing strategies for each of its products. It is very unusual for every product produced by a firm to have an identical marketing strategy. The strategy for a new product entering a competitive market and facing severe competition from rival products is likely to be different from that of a well established product which dominates a mature market. Nevertheless, there ought to be a common thread running through each strategy. This common link is a relationship to the overall strategy of the firm. If the overall strategy of the firm is to establish itself as a market leader in all its fields of operation, for example, then the marketing strategies for each of its products must reflect that aim. Different products, however, may require different strategies to reach this target. The strategy chosen for a particular product or business area will be absolutely crucial to its success. Ultimately, it may not matter what the price is or where the product is distributed if the strategy itself is wrong. Firms competing in declining markets or with a weak competitive position will struggle whatever they do. By comparison, firms which have identified strong growth areas, which build on their skills and assets are more likely to succeed. If the strategy is correct (e.g. to focus on the cheaper end of the market through permanently low prices or to extend the product overseas) good **tactical decisions** should follow on naturally.

Some different strategies

The Ansoff matrix

Some of the more common marketing strategies are illustrated by the Ansoff matrix (figure 2.1).

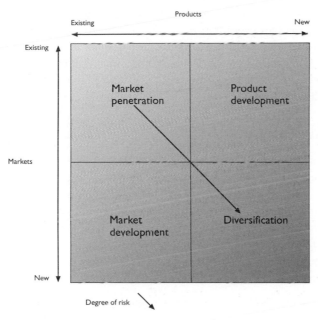

Figure 2.1 The Ansoff matrix

Market penetration

Market penetration is when a firm increases its share of a market in which it already operates. This is considered by many to be a relatively safe strategy: the firm is working in areas where it already has some knowledge, experience and understanding. Whether it wishes to increase its market share by finding new customers for the product, taking existing customers from other firms in the market or encouraging its existing customers to use its product more often, will depend on the individual circumstances of the firm. In highly competitive markets taking customers from other firms may, at best, meet with only temporary success and may provoke an aggressive reaction. The most common strategy to adopt in a competitive market is, therefore, to encourage more use from existing customers. To do this, firms can develop loyalty schemes, as many super-markets and high street shops have done, or work on promoting brand loyalty, either through the quality of the product or by creating a positive image.

Market development

This strategy involves finding new markets for the products a firm already makes. This new market could take the form of a different geographical area; a firm may decide to export products. Alternatively, it is possible to reposition a product to appeal to a new market segment, as football clubs have done to attract women and families to matches. There is a clear risk involved: the firm will not be familiar with new markets and customers. It will have to rely on external research into the market, rather than on its own experiences, so the **confidence levels** associated with its forecasts will be much lower. Despite the risks, the rewards for successfully establishing a product in a new market are likely to be proportionately higher than the rewards for increasing the product's market share through a penetration strategy.

Diversification

These two strategies both involve the firm going into new markets which are totally different from those targeted by the existing activities of the firm. It is likely to be a response to threats in its traditional areas of operation. For example, board game manufacturers are increasingly finding the threat from electronic games difficult to cope with and, as a response, have moved into other areas of operation to increase their chance of survival.

Product development

This strategy involves the improvement of products over time to maintain their competitive position. A product can be developed by changing the existing product slightly, as Mars have done recently with their new taste Mars bar, or by the introduction of new, spin-off products, such as the Mars bar ice cream which was developed in the 1980s. This strategy is particularly relevant to firms in a highly competitive situation where there is a need to have products that are different and better than those of competitors. **Brand differentiation** is what allows Heinz to charge much more for a tin of baked beans than a similar, own label product.

FACT FILE

Manchester United, the UK's biggest football club, played its first match in China in 1999. The fixture was the latest part of its campaign to go global. 'We are looking to extend the Manchester Utd brand and merchandising into Asia,' said Michael Farnan, managing director of Manchester United International, the arm set up to build the club's business worldwide. Old Trafford megastores, which stock the club's merchandise, bring in new club members, operate soccer clubs and provide cafes to watch games live, are planned for cities across Asia.
Financial Times 21 July 1999

KEY TERM

Confidence levels
the level of certainty that can be applied to forecasts based on sample results.

FACT FILE

In the late 1990s after a disappointing performance, Marks and Spencer set up a new division to research and develop business ideas outside its core operations. One of its first ideas was for Marks and Spencer to move into the telecommunications market and sell mobile phones in conjunction with Orange and Motorola.
Financial Times 13 September 1999

PROGRESS CHECK

Questions

1 Explain what is meant by a marketing strategy.
2 Using your own examples distinguish between market penetration, market development, product development and diversification strategies.

Selecting a strategy

In reality, a firm is not free to choose any marketing strategy. It would be highly unrealistic for a small, local firm with limited resources to attempt to develop new markets abroad. It would have neither the capital nor the expertise to do so successfully. Before determining its marketing strategy, then, the firm ought to consider the three general factors:

1 *The business strategy*: the marketing strategy has to be part of the firm's overall business strategy. This business strategy refers to the medium or long-term future targets of the company. It also implies that there has been careful consideration of the direction in which decision-makers wish to take the firm. Only when this overall direction has been determined can the marketing strategy be set. A business strategy that can be summarised as 'we aim to be number one in our field' could suggest a marketing strategy of penetration rather than diversification.
2 *The firm's strengths*: every firm has strengths and weaknesses. A positive brand image is a powerful asset in the marketplace, and could be used by a firm which is designing its marketing strategy. If, on the other hand, a firm has developed

a reputation for poor quality products, it would be facing an uphill battle to compete on quality, no matter how good its newer products were. Successful marketing strategies are likely to be asset-based in that they will use the firm's strengths as their basis whilst at the same time attempting to rectify perceived weaknesses. This must be taken together with the general principle of consumer orientation – it is not enough to produce the goods you are good at producing unless they also meet the needs of consumers.

3 *The market situation*: firms operate in a dynamic market situation. It is impossible for a firm to stand still, hoping that everything will continue as it has done in the past, and to be successful. The development of a marketing strategy must take account of the changing situation, as well as attempting to predict what will happen in the future. The most common framework for doing this is by undertaking a SWOT analysis. The **strengths** and **weaknesses** elements refer to the firm itself, and would be the basis of the firm's asset-led approach to its marketing strategy. The other two aspects of the SWOT analysis, the **opportunities** and **threats**, involve considering the wider environment of the firm. The opportunities which are realistically open to the firm will often limit the available marketing strategies. The threats are likely to impose even greater restrictions. A large firm diversifying to compete in a market may have a reputation for high quality products, and is also likely to be able to cross subsidise its new products with savings from economies of scale. A competing firm is then going to be faced with the threat of high quality, low price goods entering the marketplace. How should this firm compete? Reduce prices? Develop newer, better products quickly? Or diversify and spread the risks? Careful analysis should help this firm to develop an appropriate strategy, instead of having to react to a potentially devastating problem as it happens.

PROGRESS CHECK

Analyse the features of an effective marketing strategy.

There is no perfect marketing strategy. Each situation demands a different strategy in response to the circumstances. A middle ranking firm in a highly competitive market may struggle to become the market leader. Price competition is unlikely to be a viable option. Perhaps this firm may try to develop brand loyalty, or attempt to broaden its areas of operation through diversification. The key principle must be to develop the firm's existing strengths and try to eliminate its weaknesses, whilst still providing the consumer with the products they wish to buy and taking account of the external environment in terms of opportunities and threats. In short, the marketing strategy must be *realistic* for a particular firm in its specific circumstances at the time.

A successful strategy provides a match between a firm's internal strengths and external market opportunities.

Niche and mass marketing

A specific marketing strategy issue is the extent to which a firm can target its products at particular aspects of the whole market. Mass marketing involves the development of products and promotional campaigns to appeal to all types of consumer. It is usually contrasted with niche marketing which targets a specific kind of consumer.

There are several commonly held views regarding niche and mass marketing which are rather simplistic and, as a result, can be misleading. An analysis of this aspect of marketing strategy must take a realistic and balanced view of these issues:

■ '*Niche markets are short term*' – a common view of niche markets is that once the potential of a small market segment has been identified and exploited by a small firm, larger firms will enter the market and absorb it into their own mass operations. Clear examples exist in the rise and fall of Sock Shop, which found its niche of specialised socks and associated products overtaken by competition from larger clothing retailers. However, there are examples of niches that have persisted over time. Harley-Davidson Motorcycles occupy the same small market segment today as they have for many years – the mass producers of motorcycles have not produced a product which fulfils the same demand from consumers. Similarly Morgan Cars has its own special place in the hearts of car enthusiasts and can boast a 6 year waiting list for its products, despite the existence of many other cars of a similar nature. In addition, there are many examples of products which started life as niche goods but then went on to develop their own mass markets. Coca Cola, for example, was sold by its chemist inventor as a medical product, long before it became one of the world's most recognisable brands. Luxury ice creams, like Haagen Dazs or Ben and Jerry's, developed from a niche to a mass market in the same way. It is possible to find long-term success as a niche marketing firm.

■ '*Mass marketing is less risky than niche marketing*' – niche marketing does appear to be inherently risky, despite the examples of long-term success shown above. By definition, there will only be a limited number of sales in the niche, so each product has to contribute heavily to the costs and profit of the firm, implying a high price. In times of an economic recession, it may be that consumers will switch their spending to lower priced substitutes from mass marketers, effectively making the niche market uneconomic. If the niche marketer is a small firm, this may also force the firm out of business. However, mass marketing firms also face similar problems in coping with the actions of competitors and the impact of the economic climate on their operations. A well chosen portfolio of niche products could ensure the long-term survival of a firm, whilst reliance on a single mass market could be a doomed strategy. In short, all business ventures are risky, and the same principles of good management and informed planning (together with a dose of good fortune) are required for any firm to survive, whether they are niche or mass marketers.

■ '*Niche markets are for small firms*' – the product portfolios of many large companies include smaller, niche products. These may be kept on to complement other products in the firm's range, because they give the firm an entry to a growing market segment or just to reduce the level of competition. Large car manufacturers usually carry a range of products, from small cars for the town and city, through family saloons and estates, to luxury saloons, off-road and sports cars. The variations in models, as well as the additional features available for each model, allows the manufacturer to target individual segments of the total market. Indeed, many manufacturers are working towards customised features, such as trim and colour, to meet the specific needs of each individual customer. Flexible manufacturing makes this possible: you will be able to have your own personalised vehicle delivered within days of ordering it at the showroom. Similarly, many large firms in other markets adopt a niche approach to their product development. Cadbury try to cover many different segments of the chocolate market, Kellogg's do the same with breakfast cereals. So, although a niche is one way that a new, small manufacturer can gain a foothold in the marketplace, niches also hold the key for many large firms who wish to cover their whole market.

KEY TERM

SWOT analysis
involves a detailed examination of a firm's internal position and the external environment. The initials represent:
- S = Strengths
- W = Weaknesses
- O = Opportunities
- T = Threats.

S and W are *internal* to the firm.
O and T are *external* to the firm.

Questions

PROGRESS CHECK

1 Is mass marketing necessarily better than niche marketing?
2 In what circumstances might a niche marketing strategy lead to long-term success?

Competitive strategies

Whatever market strategy a firm adopts, it will have to be prepared to exist within a *competitive* marketplace. This is assumed to be the case in a mass market but, as we have already seen, it applies equally to firms in a niche market. In essence, there are two elements on which firms can compete: price and product features. Attention to both issues is important to successful marketing, but the key lies in achieving the right balance between the two. The following features must be considered carefully if the firm is going to achieve the correct price–product balance.

Product image

Some products have an associated image or status which the producer must maintain to be successful. Fashion wear relies, to a great extent, on its exclusivity to retain a market position. A competitive, price-cutting strategy for Gucci or Armani would seriously undermine their market image and threaten their market position. Consumers may be wary of purchasing such cut price items; price may be part of the status symbol image. On the other hand, mass market products would struggle if firms attempted to charge a premium price. In developing a marketing strategy, firms must be aware of the product's image and positioning within the market – selecting an unsuitable strategy could destroy the product's ability to compete.

Degree of brand loyalty

Would the market support differentiated products? In many markets the answer is

FACT FILE

McDonald's bases its marketing strategy on a clear understanding of its customers, using in-depth quantitative and qualitative customer research, and a thorough analysis of competitors. Competitors are considered in a broad way. Three areas of competition are identified: the Total Eating Out Market (covering all possibilities such as restaurants and pubs); the Quick Service Restaurant sector (including fish and chip shops and sandwich bars); and the Burger House sector (such as Burger King and Wimpy).

FACT FILE

In the late 1990s, British Airways launched a cut price airline called Go! which posed a major threat to other discount operators such as Easy Jet, Ryan Air and British Midland.

clearly yes. In supermarkets across the country, cheaper own brand products still play a relatively minor role against big name brands, even though these products may be very similar or even identical. Products as diverse as tomato ketchup, fish fingers and tinned fruit are sold under well known brand names which are able to compete successfully against similar, cheaper brands. Nevertheless, the fact that a product is differentiated in the eyes of the consumer does not automatically guarantee survival against cheaper opposition. The 'own brands' have made big in-roads to many established markets in which purchasing decisions are less frequent and require more thought; car manufacturers have suffered at the hands of cheaper imports from overseas manufacturers and exclusive shops often lose market share to high street chains. A marketing strategy must take into account the potential of differentiating the product, whilst at the same time competing with the appeal of cheaper rivals.

Sales outlets

When deciding on a competitive strategy, firms ought to take account of *where* their product is sold, in much the same way as they consider the product's image. High street chain stores may carry several similar, competing products. Can a firm differentiate its product sufficiently to allow it to charge a higher price, or will the product be seen as more expensive for no extra value? On the other hand, the firm is not likely to be successful if it competes on price in exclusive shops, such as Harrods. The customers attracted to such shops are likely to be more concerned with image and quality than price.

Existing profit margins

In a situation of fierce competition, it is possible that many, if not all, producers are already trading on very low profit margins. Price cuts may not be a viable option in the long term as they may threaten the very existence of the business. To compete in such a situation, firms have to find ways to make their product stand out from the rest. In short, firms must differentiate their product from all the others to attract new and repeat custom.

Conclusion

How useful is strategic marketing?

A simple answer to this question would be that strategic planning is vital to any firm's long-term existence. Of course, some firms exist and thrive without clear plans for the future and without knowing which direction the firm is heading. They tend to react to the external environment, rather than plan ahead. This provides flexibility, but may lead to a response which is not well co-ordinated or thought out.

It is also true that even firms with the best laid strategy do not necessarily succeed or survive. Market conditions can change very rapidly, removing a firm's competitive advantage. Nevertheless, in the vast majority of cases, competent strategic marketing is a necessary ingredient for the future success of the firm. This is because:

1 Planning gives the firm an overall direction for its marketing decisions. The marketing strategy may not give detailed instructions for every eventuality, but it does give decision-makers a clear framework within which to make their decisions. There will still be times when a decision has to be made quickly in the face of changing circumstances, but instead of making a blind guess as to the best way forward, the existence of a strategic marketing plan will act as a guide.

2 Devising a strategy forces the firm to assess its own situation in relation to its marketplace. The SWOT analysis allows the firm to be prepared for both the worst that could happen (the Threats) and the best (the Opportunities). A comprehensive SWOT analysis should reduce the chance of having to face a completely unforeseen set of circumstances, thereby allowing the firm to continue moving in its chosen direction, even when its environment is changing radically.

3 A strategy allows rational decisions to be made on the basis of the firm's overall aims and objectives. The marketing strategy is one way of ensuring that all areas of the firm are moving in the same direction and aiming for the same targets.

4 The marketing strategy is also a useful reference point for developing future plans. Changing circumstances may dictate that the existing strategy is no longer appropriate, but the plan will provide a starting point from which the firm can develop fresh ideas and a new, more relevant strategy.

In the vast majority of cases, therefore, a marketing strategy is necessary for a firm to be successful in the marketplace. The better quality the strategy, the more chance the firm has of success.

Planning resources

Firms must consider the resources they will need during the planning process and afterwards as they carry out the plan. They must also ensure that they retain as much flexibility as possible. The planning process itself can actually waste resources and firms can end up pursuing plans which are no longer appropriate for changed market conditions. Bearing this in mind, some commentators believe a firm should set an overall marketing goal without specifying too closely a particular strategy. This leaves individual brand managers or marketing managers free to develop their own plans quickly and in response to the ever changing nature of their markets. Having said this, the process of strategic planning forces people to think ahead – a useful exercise, provided the firm does not get locked into a plan which turns out to be inappropriate or dated.

KEY POINTS

A firm is more likely to undertake niche marketing when:

- major firms do not compete in the identified segment
- the firm has a unique selling proposition
- there are barriers to entry
- there are high levels of customer loyalty.

KEY POINTS

Firms are most likely to develop a successful competitive marketing strategy if they:

- know what competitors are doing
- know what consumers want
- know their own strengths
- know their own objectives.

PROGRESS CHECK

Examine the possible benefits of strategic marketing planning.

Summary chart

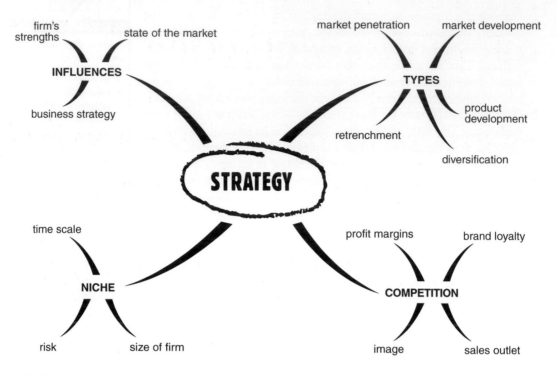

Figure 2.2 Key elements of marketing strategies

Approaching exam questions: Marketing strategies

Assess the factors a small firm might take into account when devising a marketing strategy.

(11 marks)

The key word to answering this question is 'assess'. This implies that each factor you raise not only has to be explained, but must also be weighed up, either in terms of its relative importance to the issue or its broader consequences.

The general points that you may wish to raise are:

■ the overall strategy or aims of the firm

■ the current market situation in which the firm finds itself

■ the firm's existing strengths and weaknesses.

(These last two points could be usefully considered alongside each other in a SWOT analysis.) However, since the question specifies a *small* firm, you must ensure that you address the particular situation faced by a small firm. You could also address the following points, which would not necessarily be relevant to a discussion of larger firms:

■ attitudes of managers and owners

■ skills of managers

■ whether there is a separate marketing department, or whether the marketing strategy is merely implied by the business plan

■ information available to a small firm

■ the opportunity cost of the time and money required to plan properly.

Since the question also includes the word 'might', there is no compulsion to cover every possible aspect of the topic that you can think of. In fact, the better answers often cover only a few, well chosen points, rather than attempting to cover everything. More thought can be given to each point, and everything can be made relevant to the particular case, such as the small firm in this question.

Preston Bros. produce hand-crafted furniture for the mail order market only. Discuss the strengths and weaknesses of such a niche marketing strategy.

(11 marks)

As the question asks you to discuss the strengths and weaknesses, you need to develop your points in some depth. In addition, since the question specifies strengths AND weaknesses, you must ensure you cover both sides of the discussion. Furthermore, since the question gives a specific situation, you must write within this context: make sure that the points you raise apply to this particular firm.

The issues that you may cover are:

■ Strengths

1 As the firm is probably small, a niche market allows it to concentrate on just one thing, rather than spreading itself too wide.
2 The output is likely to be high quality and can be tailored to meet the specific needs of customers.
3 A reasonable assumption would be that the firm (the brothers?) is skilled in the art of furniture manufacturing, either by training or as a hobby. Either way, they are likely to be highly motivated and dedicated to their work.
4 There may be scope for easy expansion if demand begins to grow – the firm will probably have a full range of tools, for example, but given the nature of the work may only use them sporadically. Extra labour would, therefore, not necessarily incur extra capital costs.

■ Weaknesses

1 There could be an over reliance on a single outlet, making the firm vulnerable to competition, the loss of mail order contracts or an economic downturn.
2 The firm may not be able to resist being taken over by larger competitors.
3 Loss of a single worker, perhaps through illness, may result in an inability to meet orders on time and a consequent loss of future orders.

Analyse the possible impact on an existing firm's marketing strategy of the entry of a large, multinational company to the market.

(9 marks)

Any question that includes the word 'analyse' requires the writer to look at a topic in some depth, in particular to cover aspects of cause and effect. In this case, the examiner is looking for the circumstances in which the entry of this new firm would *cause* a change of strategy, and the *effect* that this would have on the form of the strategy. When writing the answer it is better to deal with one cause and its effect at a time, rather than considering all the causes and then outlining the overall effects they could have. In addition, since the question is not context specific (very little information is given about the firms involved) you are free to include different scenarios to support your answer.

Possible lines of argument could be:

■ The new entrant may be perceived as such a major threat that the firm adopts a strategy of diversification, or even retrenchment, to avoid direct confrontation.

■ The existing firm may fight the new entrant on price or, more likely, by building brand loyalty, to maintain its market share.

■ The firm may wish to develop new, innovative products to keep ahead of the new entrant.

■ The existing firm may not perceive the threat, or may not respond quickly enough, implying no change to the marketing strategy. There are obvious dangers involved in this.

Given the potential threat posed by a large entrant to the market, the conditions under which the existing marketing strategy was devised will have changed, suggesting that it is very important for the marketing strategy to be adapted accordingly.

Evaluate the arguments for and against competing on the basis of product differentiation rather than price.

(11 marks)

The term 'evaluate' in a question implies that you must present evidence and arguments on both sides of the case and then weigh them up to arrive at a balanced and reasoned judgement. In this case, the question itself dictates what the two sides must be, so the structure of your writing ought to follow the pattern of arguments for, arguments against and an evaluation.

Arguments for include:

■ Product differentiation has a long-term focus.

■ It allows larger profit margins.

■ A differentiated brand can be used as a platform for launching future products.

Arguments against include:

■ Differentiated products can fall victim to 'me too' products.

■ Competing on price could remove opposition from the marketplace.

■ For many products, consumers are more concerned with price than image.

Overall, the final decision will depend on the particular circumstances of the firm. Is it a market leader? Does it already have strong brands? Is the market for fast moving consumer goods, where price is likely to be quite important, or for status products, where image may be more central to consumers' buying behaviour? In different circumstances either approach could be equally valid.

Student answers

Analyse the factors that could cause a firm to abandon a successful marketing strategy.

(9 marks)

Student answer

A successful marketing strategy can be the way forward for a business, but could also prevent a firm from taking advantage of new opportunities. It is important to note that a business operates in an ever changing environment. The right strategy for today's market might not be the right one for a new set of circumstances. For example, a strategy to develop an exclusive image for a brand may be inappropriate if a competitor comes up with a better product or one that is able to generate an image of higher quality.

The firm as a whole may decide to change its business objectives. Since the marketing strategy is based on the firm's objectives, a change in the objectives ought to lead to a development of the marketing strategy and, from there, to a change in the marketing plans.

So, although all firms aim to achieve a successful marketing strategy, this is not the end of the story. The marketing strategy must be under constant review to allow any necessary changes to take place.

Marker's comments

This is a good response. The student has raised two valid reasons why a marketing strategy may need to change and has made a good attempt to explain and analyse the points raised. There is a clear structure to the answer that highlights the points being made and allows a flow to develop in the argument.

Mark: Content 2/2, Application 4/4, Analysis 2/3. Total = 9

A firm has a product that has been the market leader in its segment for a number of years. Recently, its market share has been falling, although it is still the leading brand. Suggest a strategy for maintaining the brand's dominance in the long term. Justify your answer.

(9 marks)

Student answer

A firm's marketing strategy is shown by the 4P's – price, product, placing and promotion.

In this case, the product is still the market leader and it would not be wise to alter it to any great extent. It may just need modernising or developing in a minor way to keep place with competitors.

It can be assumed that the placing of the product is OK. The product is still the market leader, suggesting that it is widely available.

Depending on the prices of competitor's products, the firm may decide to amend its pricing policy. It could try to undercut competitors to develop a price advantage, or it could stay with a high price and play on its superior image.

The best course of action is likely to be with promotions – the product is still the market leader after all. Perhaps people just need reminding of the good features of the product.

Marker's comments

Despite the degree of knowledge shown by the candidate on the aspects of the marketing mix (see Chapter 6), this answer is misdirected. The marketing mix does not constitute a marketing strategy, which ought to take a broader view of the firm's products and the aims it sets for them. The candidate seems to have made an all too common error in exams: equating marketing with the marketing mix, without appreciating the broader context of this function in a business.

There are hints throughout the answer at aspects of a strategy, even if this is more by good fortune than through any direct planning on behalf of the candidate. One content mark could be awarded, but little else.

Mark: Content 1/2, Application 0/4, Analysis 0/3. Total = 1

'Niche marketers are doomed to ultimate failure.' Assess this opinion.

(11 marks)

Student answer

It is possible for a firm to exist, long term, in a niche situation, especially if the niche is too small for larger firms to be concerned about competing in it. However, this does not mean that firms in a niche market will necessarily survive for ever. Eventually, niche markets will attract the attention of competitors. If these are larger firms, they are likely to have more resources than the niche marketer, and so could compete in terms of lower prices which the niche firm may not be able to match.

Niche markets are also usually reliant on a single product. Taste and fashion may eventually turn against such products, and the niche marketer is unlikely to have other products to fall back on.

I would agree with the statement – a firm reliant on a single niche market is doomed to ultimate failure.

Marker's comments

This is a fairly good response in that it covers many appropriate points, although it is based on several assumptions. It may have been better if such assumptions, such as the small size and limited scope of the niche marketer, had been clearly stated.

The points raised, however, are connected directly to the issue in the question and are fairly well expressed. The conclusion is that the candidate fails to assess the statement and does not really add to the discussion of the points made.

Mark: Content 2/2, Application & Analysis 5/6, Evaluation 0/3. Total = 7

Assess the ways in which a firm might alter its strategy if a multinational company launched a new product in its market segment.

(11 marks)

Student answer

The launch of a new product by a multinational company is likely to be a major threat to an existing firm, whatever its status. It is likely that the product would be backed by a major promotional effort and would be capable of surviving a price war if one arose.

The existing firm, therefore, will need to be prepared to lose market share to the new competitor. The strategy options may be to develop a niche within the overall market that the multinational firm may not cover, allowing the firm to thrive, albeit in a limited way. Alternatively, the firm may abandon this market and concentrate on the other areas of operation that it may have. A third strategy may be to compete for its existing market share. Its level of success will depend on the characteristics of the firm itself.

Marker's comments

Although the answer contains many useful points, this answer is largely unbalanced. There seems to be an unwritten assumption that the firm, about which nothing is known, could not possibly compete with the multinational firm. There is no consideration of the power or otherwise of the multinational company and, although the answer hints at the possibility of competition in the final paragraph, there is no consideration of what characteristics would be useful in such a circumstance.

Mark: Content 2/2, Application & Analysis 2/6, Evaluation 0/3. Total = 4

End of section questions

1 Examine the reasons why a firm might adopt a strategy of niche marketing.

(9 marks)

2 Analyse the arguments in favour of asset-led marketing.

(9 marks)

3 Discuss the factors which might determine a firm's overall marketing strategy.

(11 marks)

4 Examine the factors that might have influenced a firm's decision to compete via lower prices.

(9 marks)

5 To what extent might a firm's existing market situation dictate its marketing strategy?

(11 marks)

6 Consider the usefulness to a firm of undertaking a SWOT analysis before determining its marketing strategy.

(11 marks)

7 Assess the possible impact the economic climate might have on a firm's marketing plans.

(11 marks)

8 Analyse the possible opportunities available to a firm wishing to increase its market share.

(9 marks)

9 Discuss the usefulness to a firm of developing a marketing strategy.

(11 marks)

10 Evaluate the arguments for and against a firm adopting a strategy of retrenchment.

(11 marks)

Essays

1 Discuss a firm's possible responses to a health scare related to its leading product.

(40 marks)

2 A large multinational airline is considering setting up a low budget operation to work in a non-traditional market. Discuss the factors it should take into account before going ahead with this plan.

(40 marks)

3 Stauder plc produces and sells glass worldwide. The company recently announced major redundancies due to the loss of several traditional markets. Produce and justify a possible strategic marketing plan that could help the firm regain its former position as a world leader.

(40 marks)

4 'The marketing strategy must be wholly determined by events in the market place'. Critically assess this statement.

(40 marks)

5 'In the long term, mass marketers will always win out over niche marketers.' Evaluate this view.

(40 marks)

Market planning

Introduction

Having determined the firm's overall aims, and transferred these into a coherent marketing strategy, the next step of the marketing process is to develop a more detailed **marketing plan**. This marketing plan will take the form of an **action plan**, identifying the activities that will be used to carry out the marketing strategy. This action plan will have three main elements:

1 the marketing activities that will be undertaken
2 the timing of actions
3 the reasons behind each action.

The marketing plan

Including each of these three elements in the marketing plan gives a document that is useful to all members of staff in the business. In particular, the marketing plan is an important tool for integrating the activities of different functions within the business. For example, the sales and production departments would both need to know the timing and likely impact of a major advertising campaign in advance so that they could adjust their own plans accordingly. The same is obviously true in reverse – the marketing plan has to reflect the work going on in other areas of the firm. The development of a new product will have an impact on the marketing plan, perhaps determining the marketing activities associated with an older product that is entering the final part of its life cycle. Plans to relaunch this product, and hence extend its life cycle, may not be appropriate in the context of the release of the new product.

The marketing plan in the context of business planning

The marketing plan is just one part of the range of action plans being developed across the whole business. All these plans should come together as a single package which reflects the overall objectives of the business. Although the importance of being consumer orientated cannot be disputed, it would not be true to say that the marketing plan is more important than all the other plans in the business. All are crucial if the firm is to achieve its overall aims and each must reflect the others so that the package works as a whole.

PROGRESS CHECK

Discuss the ways in which changes to a firm's marketing plan might affect other functions of the organisation.

Drawing up a marketing plan

In addition to the other plans in the firm and the overall strategic plan of the business, the marketing department's detailed action plan should take into account other factors as well. These will be discussed in more detail later in this chapter, but in brief they are:

- *Historical data* – all plans that people make are based on their experiences, and business planning is just the same. Previous successful plans will be analysed to see if the same actions could prove useful again. Previous failures will be avoided, although it is sensible to try to find out what went wrong. Most people, whether in business or not, prefer to stay with things that are familiar. Previous plans and previous successes often form the basis for future plans as many people are not comfortable making radical new plans with no previous experience.

- *Current trends* – marketing plans are not plucked out of thin air. They are based on the masses of data collected about the current state of the market place. What do people think of the firm's current products? Why do they buy them? How often are they bought? What are the attractions of other products in the marketplace? The answers to these and many other similar questions help a firm to decide what actions it needs to take to fulfil its objectives.

- *Future expectations* – the firm must make and take into account the best possible predictions of the future. What are the competitors going to do? Are new technological breakthroughs likely to alter the state of the market? Are new social or economic trends appearing that will change the state of the marketplace for the firm? Of course, making predictions about the future is a very inexact science for which there are no correct answers. Market plans, however, must try to look into the future if they are to be a useful document for the business.

- *Financing* – no firm has an unlimited budget for any of its activities. All marketing costs the firm. There must be a balance between the desired activities of the marketing department and the finance available from the firm. Depending on the basis used for allocating budgets, the marketing department may have a degree of flexibility for its finance. However, a clear justification is usually required for the planned amount of spending, often given in terms of the firm's strategic aims. In short, the marketing department will not be able to spend money unless it can say how it will help the firm achieve its targets.

So, a firm is not free to select any marketing plan it desires. These factors place a heavy constraint on the available options for the marketing department. The key to market planning lies in balancing the aims of the firm with the opportunities in the marketplace and the available resources.

KEY POINTS

A marketing plan is more likely to be effective if:

- it is based on good quality information
- it has an appropriate budget
- it is co-ordinated with the other functions.

PROGRESS CHECK

Analyse the factors which might influence a firm's marketing plan.

> **The six elements of marketing planning have been described as:**
> 1 looking at what has happened before
> 2 predicting what is going to happen
> 3 identifying opportunities
> 4 developing winning plans
> 5 allocating resources to their best effect
> 6 putting the plans into action.

KEY POINTS

A marketing plan is more likely to be useful if:

- the underlying data is recently gathered
- the underlying data is accurate
- managers interpret the data successfully
- the plan is realistic given the firm's resources
- it is updated to meet changing conditions.

How useful is marketing planning?

Marketing planning should co-ordinate the activities of the marketing function and ensure that individuals' efforts complement each other, rather than work against each other. For example, it should ensure a consistent message through each marketing activity. The process of planning is also extremely valuable as a means of making managers think about the future and justify their actions. In the absence of a plan it is easy to stick to the existing approach, without reconsidering the underlying assumptions and thinking about whether the present activities are suitable for the given market conditions. Planning provides an opportunity for discussion. This brings people together and helps them to develop a common vision of the future and what has to be done over the next period. Whether the plan is actually appropriate depends on the quality of the information and the ability of the management to utilise it successfully. Good information interpreted badly is as dangerous as bad information. The quality of the plan also depends on the extent to which it builds on the firm's strengths and resources. Sometimes plans can be good documents but unrealistic or inappropriate for a particular firm. Plans must be reviewed regularly to ensure they remain relevant. An inflexible plan which fails to allow a change in direction when conditions alter can be very harmful. Firms must avoid getting locked into a plan which is soon dated and misdirected.

PROGRESS CHECK

Analyse the value of marketing planning.

Do all firms have a marketing plan?

In theory, yes. In reality, no! All firms should have a clear idea of where they are heading. This means they should have an overall corporate objective and strategy. Following on from this, there should be plans for each of the different functions. Without a plan, individuals within the firm may lack any sense of priorities, and may have no understanding of what needs to be achieved or how it should be achieved. They might work very hard in their own area without actually contributing to the overall success of the firm. The corporate plan should pull together the different functional strands of the business; the marketing plan should pull together all the marketing activities. In reality, many organisations operate on a fairly informal basis when it comes to planning. The managers may have an overall view of where the business is heading, which they may or may not communicate effectively to others within the organisation. In many cases, however, this vision is not turned into a formal, detailed plan. Managers deal with problems and issues as and when they arrive, reacting rather than being proactive. As a result, many employees complain that they do not really know what they are supposed to be doing or why. They cannot plan ahead because senior managers have not provided an overall direction. This is as true within the marketing function as within the other functional areas.

One reason why some firms lack plans is because the senior managers do not see the value of them; they argue that, as the market changes all the time, they need to keep flexible. There is some merit in this argument. However, the existence of a plan, however flexible it has to be or however regularly it has to be updated, does provide a valuable source of reference for people within the firm. The lack of a plan tends to make life more uncertain for individuals and is potentially risky for firms.

Marketing budgets

On page 41, we looked briefly at the impact of financial resources on market planning. Here we consider the subject in more detail. The marketing budget sets out targets for the marketing department: how much money is available to spend as well as levels of achievements, such as sales targets and market share. It is the quantifiable aspect of the marketing plan. The figures laid down at the start of the financial year act as guidelines for the marketing department, as well as a means of control and review as the plan is running.

Budgeted v. actual

At the end of the year, the achievements of the department can be assessed. Very simply, actual and budgeted figures are compared. A favourable variance, such as an actual sales value that is greater than the budgeted one indicates a good performance by the department. A poor performance could be shown by adverse variances such as a lower than anticipated market share or greater spending on advertising. However, it is more realistic to take account of *changing circumstances*, as well as to look at actual and budgeted values. It may be that an adverse variance in sales was caused by a sudden economic downturn: perhaps all firms in the same market experienced similar problems. This actual level of sales achieved, albeit below the budgeted figure, may reflect an excellent performance given the circumstances. In the same way, a favourable variance may have been caused by factors other than the good performance of the marketing department.

KEY POINTS

The actual spending on marketing is more likely to differ from the budgeted figure if:

- the firm has changed its marketing plans
- market conditions have changed
- the firm's planning was poor
- the firm's information was inaccurate.

PROGRESS CHECK

Examine the reasons why a firm's actual spending may differ from the budgeted value.

SMART targets

A marketing budget should use targets that meet the SMART criteria (specific, measurable, agreed, realistic, time-constrained).

In this context specific means that the targets clearly identify what the aim is and what would be classed as success. Measurability implies that the targets are quantifiable. The targets need to be agreed between superiors and subordinates and set to an appropriate level. They should be realistic and achievable but not be so easy to achieve as to be relatively meaningless. Finally, the target will give an indication of the time scale involved, so that at a specific time everyone involved will be able to see whether or not the budgeted target has been achieved. For example, the strategic aim of becoming the market leader in a particular field is *not* a SMART target. The target of increasing market share from 12% to 15% by December could be SMART depending on the firm.

The value placed on marketing by a business may be reflected in the size of the finance made available for marketing, relative to the size of the firm as a whole. However highly thought of, there will always be a limit placed on the amount of money available. In essence, the size of the marketing spend should be consistent with the action plans devised to achieve the aims laid out in the marketing strategy. These, in turn, ought to reflect the overall business objectives.

> **All too often firms base their budgets on what they used to spend or what they have available, rather than on what they want to achieve.**

A recent survey found the following measures were used to assess the performance of marketing departments.

MEASURE	%	EXAMPLES
Financial	40	change in sales revenue, profit margins
Consumer	28	opinion polls, rate of usage
Market share	11	sales relative to competitors
Campaign effectiveness	9	public recognition, artistic merit
Others	12	wholesalers, employee attitudes

Table 3.1 Results of a survey of targets for marketing departments

Clearly, a strong emphasis is placed on marketing performance in terms of its financial contribution to the business as a whole. Despite the general acceptance of the idea of consumer orientation, the thoughts of consumers often take second place to the financial needs of the business. This may not be as contradictory as it appears. Money is the easiest basis on which to compare and assess performance within businesses and is one area where people believe they understand what the figures are saying. Customer orientation may be reflected in a good financial performance.

Analyse the factors which might determine the size of a firm's marketing budget.

How the marketing spend is set will vary from business to business. One of the most common methods to use is historical – allocating a figure for this year that is similar to last, perhaps with an addition to cover inflation or the growing size of the business. This assumes that last year's allocation was correct, and that little has changed. Although this method is easy to use and understand, it does go against the idea that businesses operate in a dynamic, ever changing environment. At the other extreme, a firm could use a **zero-based system** for allocating finances. This involves starting with a blank piece of paper and requires every piece of spending to be justified in terms of its contribution to the business's overall objectives. This is a fair method of allocating the limited resources of a business, but is likely to be very time consuming and can be inflexible: the funding for instant opportunities may be difficult to acquire. A compromise system may be a better option.

One such is **competitor parity**. Here a figure is allocated that is similar to the spending of comparable firms. This system, however, does mean that a firm has to have reliable information about its competitors' spending habits, and also their plans for the future. Perhaps more realistic is a system of **task-based allocations**. The marketing objectives are translated into marketing activities, each of which is then costed. This forms the basis of the money made available to the marketing department. Whatever the basis used for allocating funds to the marketing function the department must use its resources **effectively** and **efficiently**.

In order to be both effective and efficient, the marketing plan needs to be based on the best information available. As mentioned on page 41 this information is often based on previous experiences, the current state of the marketplace and forecasts of possible futures. Here we consider these aspects in more detail.

The past

Backdata

Most firms have a mass of historical data on which to draw. Past sales figures, details of pricing and promotional strategies and the results from previous market research can all be put together to form an impressive array of **backdata** which can be used as a basis for decision making. Of course, all past data should be treated with a degree of caution – the environment in which a firm is operating today is unlikely to be reflected in the circumstances of the past. However, there is still potential for using the past as a guide to the future.

Backdata can be used to interpret new market research findings. If a previous survey found that 60% of people said they would try a certain product, giving actual sales of £2 m per year, and a new survey for a similar product that found that 75% of respondents would try the product we might predict sales in excess of £2 m per year

KEY TERMS

Effective
achieving a set target.

Efficient
using only the limited set of resources (time or money) available or less.

Effective and efficient
achieving a goal within the limits of resources available.

KEY POINTS

The marketing budget is likely to be larger if:

- the firm has plans requiring a high level of funding for marketing
- the firm has a high level of financial resources
- competitors' spending is high
- the firm has had large budgets in the past
- the firm is market-orientated
- the expected returns are high.

(a perfect relationship would show an increase of a quarter, leading to a sales prediction of £2.5 m per year). The key point is that past data should not be dismissed because it is out of date, but neither should it be accepted at face value. Firms must attempt to identify the changes in the environment and to new backdata in the light of this information.

The present

Up-to-the-minute information is increasingly available given the rise of information technology. Firms can know almost instantaneously how sales are going for any of its products in any of its retail channels. Is the product selling better from large supermarkets or corner shops? Are different prices being charged and if so what is the effect this is having on sales?

The **price elasticity of demand** is a concept of growing importance for marketers. In the past, the concept has been dismissed as having little practical use due to the difficulty of obtaining accurate information from which to calculate elasticities. Today, though, marketers can see with relative ease what the effect of a change in price has been on the level of sales. It is quite possible to find out, with some degree of accuracy, what the price elasticity of demand is for any given product. For most consumer products, price is an important determining factor in any change in demand in the short term. Whilst a brand image can help establish a product and permit higher prices to be charged (for example Andrex toilet rolls compared to a supermarket's own brand) a change in the short-term level of demand can be determined by special offers and price cuts. This implies that the demand for such products is price elastic – a small fall in price often leads to a relatively large increase in demand.

For a firm, there are two main reasons for knowing the price elasticity of its products. Firstly, the concept helps to determine the pricing strategy, taking into account the costs of producing the product. Price elasticity tells a firm the effects of the different options open to it. Charging a high price to skim the top end of the market could attract few sales, but the low level of sales may be sufficient to cover costs. Penetrating a market by charging a low price may give rise to a large market share, but will the revenue cover the costs of production? And what will the effect be on sales when the price is increased to a more sustainable level? Will brand loyalty have been created so that the sales remain high, or will many sales be lost? It is worth remembering the effect price changes have on total revenue, as shown in table 3.2 below.

	PRICE ELASTIC	**PRICE INELASTIC**
Effect of price rise	Total revenue falls	Total revenue increases
Effect of price cut	Total revenue increases	Total revenue falls

Table 3.2 The effect of price changes on revenue

As well as helping to determine pricing strategy, price elasticity can help a firm to determine its sales forecasts. If the value of elasticity is known, it may be possible to predict with some accuracy what the level of sales will be following a proposed price change. Such information can be a great help to production departments, stock controllers etc., as well as to the marketing department itself.

It is important to remember that values of elasticity are estimates based either on past experience or research. The values could change over time and managers must use them with some caution.

Market testing

As part of the information-gathering process necessary for marketing planning, firms may use test markets as a means of determining the current climate for its products. In the same way that firms have used test markets for new products for many years, they are increasingly using the technique to test developments of existing products and the impact of changes in price or packaging, etc. Any market that can be isolated in some way, whether geographically (often using ITV television regions to permit local TV advertising) or by type of customer (using different outlets) can be used as a test market. It is crucial that test results can be applied to the whole of the firm's marketplace. If the test area is not typical of the whole population, the test findings will not be applicable on a larger scale. They will be of little practical value to the firm.

The future

Forecasting

It has been said that one main purpose of marketing is to anticipate the future to ensure that the organisation achieves the best possible outcome. Of course, forecasting is a very inexact science. There are so many variables and unknowns that, in some cases, the future cannot be described with much confidence. The best forecasts available at the time suggested that the Sony Walkman would be a failure – it did not address a need in the marketplace. Around the same time, the Sinclair C5 car/bike, it was predicted, would become a widely used form of transport, combining the cheapness of a bicycle with the ease of use of a motor car. Of course, both these forecasts were spectacularly incorrect.

Forecasts as a basis for planning

In spite of these examples, it is generally held that forecasts give the businesses a basis on which to plan. Sony, having been made aware of the potential limitations of the Walkman through market research, were able to devise a strategy that gave the product its best chance of success. It could be said that future plans are meaningless unless an attempt has been made to forecast the future. Sales can not be estimated without knowing something of the probable economic environment that the firm will be facing in the future. Is the firm likely to face more competitors? Is it true that a main rival is considering retrenchment away from the firm's operations?

KEY POINTS

The price elasticity of demand for a product or service is likely to be higher if:

- there are similar, substitute products on the market
- it is easy to switch from one product to another
- it is not heavily branded
- it is not highly differentiated (e.g. there is no USP)
- it is a shopping good (one which consumers 'shop around' for)
- price is a key factor in the buying decision.

KEY POINTS

Findings from a test market are more likely to be useful if:

- the test market is representative of the whole population
- the findings are interpreted accurately
- competitors do not take actions to invalidate the findings
- by delaying a national launch the firm does not lose the first-mover advantage (being first into the marketplace).

How will the firm react if these events happen? By undertaking forecasts that take into account such factors, the firm can plan its marketing activities with much more confidence.

Market forecasting also has an impact on other areas of the business, such as workforce planning, operations scheduling and financial planning. The value of a forecast depends on the quality of the data on which it was based and the methods used. **Extrapolation**, for example, projects past trends forwards; this is only likely to be accurate if the market conditions have not changed greatly. A forecast based on intuition or gut feeling, by comparison, may predict sudden changes which extrapolation might miss. However, this is a more risky strategy.

PROGRESS CHECK

Questions

1 How useful are sales forecasts?
2 Examine how a firm might set its marketing budget.

Summary chart

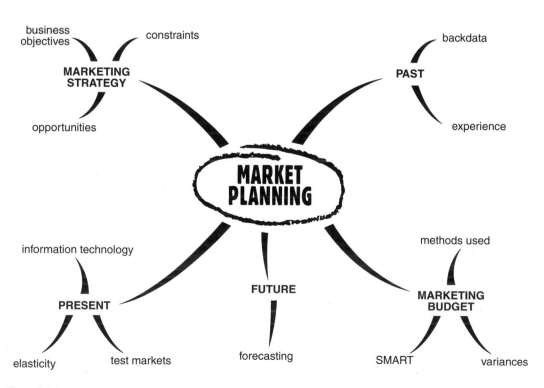

Figure 3.1 Key elements of market planning

Approaching exam questions: Market planning

'Small firms with no marketing department cannot be involved in market planning.' Discuss this view.

(40 marks)

As with all questions that contain the instruction 'discuss', this one is expecting a two-sided answer. What is there about this statement that is true, and what is there that is not true? Also implied in the question is the need to arrive at a reasoned conclusion; the final evaluation is likely to be along the lines of 'this statement is true to a certain degree but ...'

When writing an answer to a question like this, you must be careful to restrict your answer to the context (here small firms) specified in the question. There will be little credit gained for demonstrating a sound knowledge of how market planning takes place in a large firm.

To agree with the statement, you may consider discussing some of the following points:

- the lack of resources to conduct market research

- the lack of time and resources for gathering full data on current sales

- the possible lack of specialist expertise

- the lack of a formal planning process in small firms.

Against the statement you might raise some of the following points:

- Whether formal or not, market plans are developed by all firms; all businesses take pricing decisions, decide on advertising and promotions, etc.

- Small does not always imply a lack of specialists.

- It has been argued that small firms must be successful marketers in order to survive.

Following your discussion of these or similar points, you must produce a conclusion or evaluation with a justification. This will be determined by the points you have raised, but may highlight the need for marketing skills, including marketing planning, for the long-term survival of the firm, whether these skills are put to use to produce a formal written document or just implied by actions.

Assess the usefulness of the concept of price elasticity to a firm selling luxury cars.

(40 marks)

The term 'assess' in an essay style question indicates that depth is required for each of the points considered. As with most essays, candidates should consider two sides before arriving at a balanced conclusion. An analysis of the usefulness of a technique requires points to be made, both in support of the benefits of the technique and also highlighting any limitations it may have.

Support for the use of elasticity could include some of the following points:

■ If the product is a luxury it is likely to be price inelastic. This knowledge allows the firm to focus more on issues that could significantly affect demand.

■ If the basic information is correct, elasticities allow the firm to make relatively accurate decisions about such things as pricing.

■ Basing decisions on any hard data must be better than using guess work.

■ Modern IT is making the technique more available and more reliable.

Factors against using elasticity could be:

■ As luxuries are perceived as being price inelastic, firms may mistakenly assume that price is of *no* importance.

■ Despite advances in Information Technology, elasticities change so quickly the data is always going to be unreliable.

■ The market place changes too quickly to make any prediction based on historic data safe.

■ Managers can be fooled into believing elasticities are accurate, purely because the methods of calculation used appear scientific. This can lead to an over reliance on dubious data.

On balance, the technique may be said to be useful if applied with a degree of caution. It should not be used in isolation from other forecasting techniques, which may take into account wider contextual issues.

Assess the problems that may be faced by a newly formed business which is gathering information on which to base its marketing plan.

(40 marks)

The directive to 'assess' issues requires students to come to some form of judgement on each of the identified problems. The judgement could be about the degree of severity of each problem, or the extent to which the solution lies within the grasp of the firm.

As with most essay type questions, a context is provided. In this case, the discussion ought to centre around the specific problems faced by a newly formed business, rather than looking generally at the problems that could be faced by any firm. Some of the relevant issues you may consider are:

■ *A lack of past experience* – this could cause problems. However, just because the business is new, it does not necessarily mean that the people running the business are new to the field – a new business may take the form of a management buy-out or may have been set up by workers who have been made redundant from a similar firm.

■ *A lack of finance* – new firms generally do not have a lot of spare capital, although they may feel that market research is of sufficient importance to give it a proportion of the available resources.

■ *A lack of expertise in collecting and interpreting research data* – however, similar issues could be raised as with the apparent lack of experience. It is possible to outsource market research to draw on the expertise of others, although there is clearly a financial cost associated with this.

Since the question includes the word 'may' you can include a degree of speculation in your answer, such as whether or not the people setting up the new business have past experience in this field or not. However it is vital that you both state any such assumption and acknowledge that they will not always be the case.

'Plans are made about the future, which by definition is unknown. This makes those plans at best unsafe and at worst a liability to the firm.' Evaluate the importance of planning to a marketing department in a multinational firm.

(40 marks)

As the question asks you to evaluate a proposition, you need to present arguments for both sides of the case and then arrive at a clear judgement about how important, or otherwise, planning is in this context. Given the scenario of a multinational firm, the points that can be raised are much broader in scope than in the case of a small firm.

Possible issues that could be raised are:

- the need for co-ordination between different functions or different geographical regions
- the need for the diverse plans from different areas to be consistent in terms of addressing the overall business objectives
- the availability of large quantities of data on which to base plans.

However, the firm must be aware of potential problems such as

- information overload
- the non-transferability of findings between different geographical regions
- the scale of the co-ordination problem across different areas of the world.

It may be a reasonable conclusion that, despite the clear problems involved in market planning, businesses need to make the attempt so that they have something on which to base future action. Such planning ought not, though, be taken in isolation from other factors.

Student answers

Discuss the factors that may constrain a firm's marketing plan.

(9 marks)

Student answer

A firm's marketing plan may be limited by several factors:

- *Finance* – the overall amount of available money will limit the amount that can be spent on advertising and so on.

- *Competition* – the activities of competitors will influence the choices a firm can make.

- *Aims* – the firm's aims will have to be taken into account when setting a marketing plan.

- *Market research* – the plan ought to be based on available information, and the more limited the data, the more limited the plan.

- *Products* – the plan has to be realistic to the firm's products.

Marker's comments

The use of bullet points is usually not a good way of developing detail and depth in an answer. It tends to limit the development of the points being made. In this case, there are five useful points made, but none are developed beyond a single line. A better use of the limited time available in an exam would be to raise fewer points but to cover each one in more depth.

Mark: Content 2/2, Application 1/4, Analysis 0/3. Total = 3

Examine the ways in which the performance of a marketing department can be measured.

(9 marks)

Student answer

There are several ways in which the performance of the marketing department can be measured.

Firstly, a simple profit measure can be used. If the aim of the firm is to make a profit, the aim of the marketing department must be to put into place a policy that allows the firm to make that profit. The more profitable the firm, the better the marketing department must be doing.

Secondly, the firm could use attitude surveys to find out if the marketing department is actually developing the image of products successfully with consumers. This is particularly important if the products are similar to those of competitors, meaning that the marketing department has to be able to differentiate their products in the minds of consumers.

The measure chosen will have to be clearly linked to the aims set for the marketing department. It is only fair to use a target that the marketing department can measure and can achieve.

Marker's comments

This is a fair response in that it clearly expresses the central theme of the answer within the context of the question asked. The points are relevant to the debate and, as such, attract content marks. Although they are not really analysed in a great depth, there is still direction to the answer and it gains a good mark.

Mark: Content 2/2, Application 3/4, Analysis 2/3. Total = 7

Analyse the different ways in which a marketing budget may be set.

(9 marks)

Student answer

A marketing budget can be set on two main bases:

1 *Historical* – this means setting a budget in line with the budget set in previous years. It assumes that little will have changed from one year to the next, and so may not always match the current needs of the marketing department. Since marketing takes place in a dynamic environment it is likely that many factors will change, meaning that a historical budget will not meet the actual needs of the marketing department.
2 *Zero-based* – this means that the budget starts from nothing, and the marketing department has to justify all the money given to it by the firm in terms of its current needs and future plans. Although this is likely to be more accurate in the long run, it can be very time-consuming and complex to set up. It can also lead to resentment if the carefully calculated budget is amended by the firm when it has received bids from all the other departments as well.

In an ideal situation, a compromise can be found between the two methods, allowing some historical base while still tailoring the budget to meet current needs.

Marker's comments

Although an answer in point form is usually unwise, in this case the student has been able to develop his or her first point fully before moving on to the second. It is pleasing to note that the issues are raised and that there is a real attempt to link the answer to the question set. The final evaluation provides a useful ending to the discussion. Although it could usefully have been extended, there are sufficient elements of judgement throughout the answer to merit a high mark for evaluation.

Mark: Content 2/2, Application 4/4, Analysis 2/3. Total = 8

Evaluate the usefulness of the concept of price elasticity of demand.

(11 marks)

Student answer

Price elasticity of demand tells a firm how much the demand for its products is likely to change in response to a change in price. It is important for a firm to have this information when it is planning its pricing strategy. It would be no good if the firm changed its price and found out that as a consequence that it actually lost revenue.

The idea of elasticity of demand is therefore a crucial one for a firm when it is considering changing its prices.

Marker's comments

Although this is a fair answer, it is very limited in scope. Questions such as this always require a two-sided response – this answer illustrates the usefulness of the concept, but does not consider its limitations in any way.

Mark: Content 2/2, Application & Analysis 2/6, Evaluation 0/3. Total = 4

End of section questions

1 Examine the possible impact of developments in information technology on forecasting.

(9 marks)

2 Examine the features of an effective marketing plan.

(9 marks)

3 Discuss the possible value of test markets in devising a marketing plan.

(11 marks)

4 Analyse the factors which might be taken into account when devising a marketing plan.

(9 marks)

5 To what extent is price elasticity a useful concept for market planning?

(11 marks)

6 Consider the usefulness of market planning.

(11 marks)

7 To what extent should a marketing plan be based on the past?

(11 marks)

8 Analyse the use of variances as a means of assessing a marketing department's performance.

(9 marks)

9 Discuss the usefulness of setting a marketing budget.

(11 marks)

10 Evaluate the usefulness of setting SMART targets.

(11 marks)

Essays

1 To what extent should a marketing budget be determined by competitors' spending?

(40 marks)

2 'Given the rate of change in markets nowadays, marketing planning is largely a waste of time.' Discuss this view.

(40 marks)

3 Sometimes firms ignore the results of their own market research. Justify such an approach.

(40 marks)

4 'A marketing plan should look to the future and disregard the past.' Critically assess this statement.

(40 marks)

5 Evaluate the arguments for and against a small firm engaging in long-term market planning.

(40 marks)

Market research

Introduction

Market research is the process a business goes through to find out about its actual and potential customers. If you accept the commonly held view that businesses ought to be market or customer orientated, it follows that market research has to be the starting point for business decision-making. Decisions on how best to serve the market can only be made accurately if the needs and wishes of the market can be taken into account.

KEY TERM

Market research
involves the gathering, analysing and presenting of information relevant to the marketing process.

> **Market research aims to reduce risk by providing managers with the information they need to make better decisions.**

The function of market research

In one sense, market research is all about reducing risk. The more information a firm has, the more likely it is to make appropriate decisions concerning its marketing activities. Despite these simple conclusions, there are many examples of firms which undertake insufficient or inappropriate research. Some firms do not fully appreciate the market research function. However, it is also true that the sheer complexity of people and their behaviour make research very difficult. Psychologists would argue that it is impossible to achieve a full understanding of a market because of the contradictions inherent in human beings and their social interactions. Nevertheless, businesses have to try to understand their market as fully as possible if they are to have the best chance possible to survive and prosper.

KEY POINTS

Organisations which undertake market research are more likely to know:

- how consumers evaluate their products or services against those of competitors
- what consumers are looking for in this market and how far the firm is providing this effectively
- how consumer tastes are changing
- what consumers are buying from whom and why
- how consumers will react to new ideas the firm has thought up
- the extent of customer loyalty and retention.

Strategic and tactical research

Firms ought to be aware that market research comes in two forms, strategic and tactical.

1 *Tactical research* – most of the research that is carried out by businesses is tactical in nature. It tries to find out how consumers would react to a particular product or a product's name, inquiring after the buying habits of customers or potential customers.

2 *Strategic research* – this, on the other hand, takes a long-term perspective by looking at market segmentation or attitude surveys. This allows firms to build

up a clear picture of motivations and the issues underlying the behaviour of customers.

Many firms tend to concentrate on tactical research, looking for short-term solutions to short-term problems and issues. It may be that, if more attention was paid to the bigger picture, better long-term decisions would be made, giving firms a clear competitive advantage.

PROGRESS CHECK

Explain why many firms tend to rely on tactical market research.

Gathering data is not enough. Managers have to interpret this data to turn it into information. Information not data helps decision-making.

The importance of market research

It appears self-evident that market research carried out by the marketing department is of great importance to a firm. But how does it compare to the importance of the personnel or finance departments? Simplistic arguments can be put forward to stress the importance of a single aspect of a firm but, in reality, all aspects must be given sufficient weighting if the business is to succeed. Business decisions ought to be based on a sound knowledge of the marketplace, but without the right people to carry forward those plans, without the finance to put them into practice and without the machinery and plant to produce the products, the market research results would count for very little.

Research v. hunch

There is a danger that managers might place too much emphasis on market research. After all, the results of market research come in the form of 'hard' data, such as numbers and graphs and the methods appear scientific. It is very tempting to believe such data and take it at face value. The people within the business, from managers down, are likely to have between them a solid body of experience in this and related industries. There must be a place in business for hunches based on experience, even if they go against the apparently 'solid' findings of market research. The example of the Sony Walkman illustrates this perfectly. The story of the product's development seems unbelievable. It is said that the Chairman of the company was always being disturbed at home by his teenage children playing their records. The children refused to wear their headphones as these prevented them from moving freely around their rooms. From this came the idea of a music player that would not disturb other people, but that would also allow the listener freedom of movement. So, although market research did not fully support the idea, the product was based on a real need. It was the product of creativity rather than the results of market research.

FACT FILE

In the 1980s, the food company Danone launched a range of yoghurts into Japan on the basis of extremely positive market research. The products failed to meet their sales targets. It later turned out that Japanese consumers had told the researchers they liked the products even when they did not because they did not want to upset them!

KEY POINTS

Managers are more likely to place too much emphasis on the results of market research if:

- the business has a culture of blame, risk avoidance, playing it safe and if the senior management style tends towards being autocratic.
- managers are not encouraged to use their initiative.
- managers lack insight into the problem.

Questions

1 To what extent would you agree that market research is only as valuable as the ability of managers to use it?
2 Consider whether market research is a safe basis for decision-making.

NUMERICAL INVESTIGATION

Market research gave the following data about snack consumption:

	UK SALES VALUE (£M)	
	1998	1994
savoury snacks	1057	633.3
crisps	909.2	909.3
snack nuts	145.5	145.5
popcorn	69.4	38.2
cereal bars	67.8	22

Table 4.1 Sales of snacks in the UK

Source: Financial Times September 22 1999

1 Show these changes using an appropriate diagram.
2 Assess the main changes.

Dangers of interpretation

So, one danger facing managers is being too reliant on market research findings. Although the figures may appear to be solid facts, the data collection methods used are often open to bias and results can be misinterpreted. Despite this, managers may feel that it is safer to rely on the data provided, than to go with their hunches or intuition. After all, if the decision turns out to have been the wrong one, they can always pass the blame on to the researchers for providing invalid information in the first place. For managers to make the best decisions, the business must be prepared to accept that honest mistakes can be made, but that it is only in an atmosphere of trust and openness that the intuitive developments, which are often the greater ones, will be made.

How important is marketing research to a firm?

How much should be spent on market research?

If it is accepted that market research is important for a firm (as long as managers are also allowed to develop their hunches), a business must ask itself how much of its limited resources should be spent on gathering the market research data. In Chapter 3 we saw that the marketing budget as a whole can be influenced by various factors; the market research budget is part of the overall marketing budget. The question should really be 'how big a part of the marketing budget should be devoted to market research?' The determinants of the answer could be:

■ the importance placed on the results of research.

■ how reliable research results have been in the past.

■ the state of the firm's market – is it changing rapidly, thereby requiring up-to-date information, or is it static?

■ the firm's strategic plan – are big changes planned or new products being launched?

As a general rule, large firms not only spend more than small ones on market research, but they also spend a larger proportion. For small firms, market research tends to come by word of mouth and entrepreneurs make generalised observations about the state of the market. Larger firms are more likely to develop formalised market research programmes which may run continuously from one year to the next.

> **No matter how much money is spent on market research, it will only be useful if the right information is available to the right people at the right time.**

PROGRESS CHECK

How much should a firm spend on marketing research?

What is the best source of market research?

Primary and secondary sources

There are several sources of research data available to a firm. Decisions have to be made about the suitability and reliability of different sources as a basis for decision-making. Two types of research data are summarised in table 4.2. Note that the benefits of one source tend to be the drawbacks of the other.

KEY POINTS

Hunch is more likely to be used if:

- gathering information is expensive and time-consuming
- the manager is a risk-taker
- the manager trusts his or her intuition
- a decision has to be taken quickly.

KEY POINTS

Market research is most likely to be useful when:

- it has been undertaken recently
- it has been undertaken by professionals
- it is primary
- the sample is large
- it is placed in context.

FACT FILE

There are many examples of major products that succeeded despite negative research findings. Post-It notes received a negative response to testing and even when the product was first launched, backed by advertising but no samples, the product was a failure. It was only when samples were given away that consumers understood what they were for. The product became 3M's biggest ever seller.

PRIMARY	SECONDARY
Relevant to the firm and its issues	Cheap to access
Follow-up research may be possible	Analysis will usually have been undertaken
The source data is available if required	The format will make the data accessible to non-specialists

Table 4.2 The advantages of primary and secondary data collection techniques

Clearly, both primary and secondary data have their uses. The best decisions usually take account of data from both types of sources. For example, the specific information derived from the firm's own primary data can be placed in a more generalised market context by reviewing secondary sources.

Sources of secondary data

There are many different sources of secondary data which may or may not be useful, depending on the question being researched by a firm. Here are some common sources consulted by businesses:

- *The government:* Annual Abstract of Statistics; Social Trends; Regional Trends; Economic Trends.

- *International Organisations:* Eurostat; OECD; IMF.

- *Bought-in services:* Mintel; Financial Times Information Service; Economist Intelligence Unit; Keynotes; Retail Business.

- *Specialist magazines:* for example The Grocer; Pig Farmer Weekly.

These sources of secondary data publish statistical and analytical information on specific market sectors or give broad data on such things as demographics and behaviour patterns. The information found in such publications is general and given in terms of the market as a whole. A firm wishing to make specific decisions will need to add to this with more detailed data to make the best decision possible.

PROGRESS CHECK

Is primary research better than secondary?

Sampling

A common concern with primary data is its reliance on the use of samples. Complete sets of data do exist, sales records for a firm for example. However, some data is collected by means such as questionnaires or observation and it is usually necessary to use some sort of sampling. Here we look at both the limitations and strengths of such techniques.

Confidence in results

When using sample data as a basis for decision-making, one of the most important pieces of information is the **confidence level** associated with the sample. This simply means the *degree of certainty* that the findings from the sample are a true

NUMERICAL INVESTIGATION

FEMALE	1992		1997 (EST.)		2002 (PROJ.)	
	000s	%	000s	%	000s	%
0–4	1,905	6	1,809	6	1,737	6
5–14	3,545	12	3,731	12	3,730	12
15–19	1,726	6	1,759	6	3,730	6

Table 4.3 Trends in the UK population, by gender and age, 1992–2002 (extract) Source: ONS/Mintel

The so-called KGOY (**Kids growing old, younger**) phenomenon, whereby children are tending to reject child-orientated things at an early age, has put pressure on traditional childrenswear manufacturers and retailers. Children as young as five are aware of brands and may refuse to wear non-branded garments or at least demand a say in the type of garments they wear. As children reach their early teens, they expect to be able to wear garments similar to that of key influencers, such as pop stars or television presenters, who may be significantly older.

The UK market for teenage clothing has risen by a healthy 22% in real terms during the period 1993–98, to stand at an estimated £2,260 m in 1998. Much of this growth is attributed to the development of designer brands and sports labels which have bolstered overall average price. The teenage girls' sector of the market accounted for 55.5% of value sales in 1997 compared with 57% in 1995, with teenage boys' clothing increasing their share of the market. This is likely to be due to the greater emphasis on branded garments within the male sector while girls tend to purchase higher amounts of retailer branded goods.

(Source: Mintel, Teenagewear Market Intelligence, June 1998)

1 As a producer and retailer of clothing for girls aged 5–14, analyse the above information and produce a suggested strategy for the next 10 years.
2 What other information might you wish to gather from primary sources?

representation of the whole population. Most market research attempts to give results at the 95% confidence level, meaning that the conclusions would be a correct representation of the whole population 19 times out of every 20. Of course, a 100% confidence level would be the ideal situation, but can only be achieved by sampling the whole population – miss out one person and you could not say with complete confidence that your results were a true reflection of the whole population.

Bearing this in mind, it seems reasonable to conclude that the bigger the sample size, the better, since the data is more likely to be representative. However, balanced against this is the cost of gathering data from larger and larger samples. It stands to reason that the more data you wish to gather, the more it costs, both in terms of collecting and analysing the data. The sample size will always be the result of a trade-off between the level of accuracy desired and the amount the firm is willing to spend. So, whilst large firms, who probably have the greatest resources available to them, may be able to undertake research in large samples, smaller firms may find themselves restricted to small samples and, therefore, a lower degree of accuracy. Nevertheless, the numbers used in sampling need not be massive. It is possible for a sample size in the hundreds to give a fair representation of most market sectors.

Even the large samples selected by organisations with relatively unrestricted budgets can be misleading. The Office for National Statistics (ONS), the body that compiles official data for the government, publishes monthly information on a variety of issues, such as the average earnings index, used by many as a guide to future rates of inflation. This is a figure which has a huge impact on many financial decisions taken in the UK such as the decision to raise or lower interest rates. In late 1998, the figures from the ONS were suspended as earlier figures, based on sample data, were found to be widely inaccurate. The gap between public and private sector pay increases, which was initially given as 2.8% turned out to be only 0.5%. Large samples do not always mean complete accuracy.

KEY POINTS

Samples are more likely to be useful if:

- they are large
- they reflect the target population
- they are cost effective
- they are relatively easy to identify and test.

PROGRESS CHECK

A survey was undertaken into the name of a new chocolate bar. A majority preferred the name 'De-lite' to the alternative 'No-fat'. The confidence level attached to the finding was 95%. What does this imply for the firm and its new product?

PROGRESS CHECK

Discuss the value of using samples in market research.

Recent developments in market research

Information Technology – the benefits

The prime development in market research in recent times, as with many other aspects of the business world, has been Information and Communications Technology. The broader impact of technology on marketing is considered in more detail in Chapter 7. The ability to gather more data, more quickly and to apply comprehensive statistical analyses has given market researchers a head start.

Collecting information

Perhaps the most significant application of Information Technology in market research relates to its ability to handle vast quantities of information. For a consumer-orientated firm, the more information that can be used to build profiles of consumers, the more able the firm will be to respond to their individual needs and demands. Many firms are making use of database-driven research. Recently, the major supermarkets, for example, have issued customers with 'loyalty cards', which they use to earn points towards rewards such as vouchers or discounts on products. A 'by-product' of these schemes is that, every time a loyalty card is used, the firm's information about that customer is increased. Over time, the firm can build up an accurate picture of what products are bought regularly and which only on occasion. The type of family can be determined – does the customer buy nappies and baby products, or meals for one? Does the customer have a pet? By obtaining such information, the firm is able to be more effective in its target marketing. Mailings can be made to specific customers for certain types of products, and stores in particular areas can undertake promotions that will appeal to the type of shopper that usually frequents the store.

PROGRESS CHECK

Questions

1 Is more information always a good thing? Explain your answer.
2 Can a firm ever be certain it has the right quantity of information? Why or why not?

Analysis of data

Information Technology provides data in detail, but also at a speed that allows firms to respond quickly to changes in circumstances. A new trend in buying habits may develop very quickly, and today's Information Technology can highlight such changes almost instantaneously. Decisions on the type of product to stock and in what quantities can, therefore, be made in time to meet the changing demand.

IT – the drawbacks

Does all this mean that businesses are better placed for success today than they were in the past? Despite the quantity of data available and the speed at which it appears, there are still limitations on the ability of firms to use market research to make the best decision every time.

> **If you gather too much information there is the danger of 'paralysis by analysis'; you spend so long analysing the data that by the time you make a decision it is too late.**

The competition

Although one firm may have better data on which to base its decisions, so will its competitors. So, in theory the existence of improved IT ought not to give any firm a significant competitive advantage. *All* the main supermarket chains will be compiling masses of information on their customers and will be able to track developing trends in buyer behaviour. The competitive advantage lies, as it always has done, on the ability to make the *best decisions* based on the data available. An emerging trend may be the start of a large change in consumer demand, or may merely be a temporary blip. The ability to decide which it is will determine which firm responds in the most appropriate fashion.

> **PROGRESS CHECK**
>
> How might a firm derive a competitive advantage from the use of modern Information Technology in its market research?

Past v. future

No matter how quickly it is produced, information always relates to events that have happened in the past. The decisions a firm has to make about its customers are about the future. It is not always easy to predict future events from past data.

It is still the case, as it always has been, that market research data alone is not a sufficient basis on which to make management decisions. Business decisions are all about predicting what circumstances will prevail in the future, and then determining the most appropriate course of action for that future. The historical data from market research may be a starting point, but is not the end of the decision-making process.

How useful is market research?

Market research can provide firms with the information they need to make better decisions. However, how useful it is depends on the accuracy and relevance of the information gathered. If the data is out of date or inaccurate, then clearly it is of limited use – indeed using it may be positively dangerous. The benefits of research must also be weighted up against the costs – it may be that the gains are not worth the effort, time and money expended and the manager would have been better to rely on experience or intuition. It is also important to remember that research simply provides information – it does not guarantee that appropriate action is taken. Managers may still follow their gut feeling whatever the research says or they may come to an information-led decision and then may not be able to implement their plan effectively. Market research can, therefore, contribute to the success of a firm, but cannot guarantee it.

PROGRESS CHECK

To what extent can market research improve a firm's competitiveness?

Making decisions

Is basing decisions on hunch or experience better than using market research? This depends on how good the hunch is or how experienced the manager is compared to the quality of the research! If the research is poor and the hunch is good, then, yes, a hunch may well be better. There are certainly occasions when hunches have paid off. In markets such as the art world, fashion design and film-making, creative hunches have sometimes set off new trends that research could not have predicted – sometimes the customers may not know what they want before they have it. Was the sudden success of the pet toy, Tamagochi, due to extensive research or was it a good product idea which happened to take off? In a rush, in a situation where there is limited data or where you are deliberately trying to do something unexpected, a hunch may serve you well. Similarly, experience can contribute a great deal to a decision and may reduce the need for extra data. Having said this, good quality data should make reaching a decision easier. Research should, therefore, be used wherever possible, assuming the expected benefits are worth the investment of time and money.

PROGRESS CHECK

When might a hunch be more useful than market research?

Summary chart

Figure 4.1 Key elements of market research

Approaching exam questions: Market research

'I know that only half of the market research data is useful, but until I collect it, I don't know which half.' Does this imply that firms ought to cut back on their spending on market research?

(40 marks)

Clearly this question requires a two-sided answer, looking at the arguments for and against cutting spending on market research, and then it needs a reasoned conclusion.

The quote in the question is often found in marketing texts as it provides a neat introduction to one of the key issues of market research: the information gathered is only as good as the use made of it. So, whilst on one side of the argument, we can say that all firms have limited resources and can not afford to waste them on research that is profitless, the other side of the argument must be that half the data is useless, not because it is poor data, but because of the analysis and decision-making that stems from it.

Issues that could be raised in this answer are outlined below.

Reasons for cutting spending:

■ Limited resources ought not to be wasted on unused research.

■ If the problems were more precisely determined before research began, then the research could be better targeted and, therefore, more useful.

■ Less research would mean less risk of information overload, allowing a better quality of decision to be made.

Arguments against cutting spending:

■ All data is potentially useful, so the more that is available the better managers' decisions are likely to be.

■ Even if data is not used for the present decision, it may be useful to determine the bigger picture for other decisions in the future.

■ Who is criticising the data? Even if one manager does not use the data, another might be relying on it.

■ If it is not known which data is going to be useful and which is not before the data is collected, then it is impossible to make a decision on how the market research is to be cut.

Although the quote in the title sounds clever and may be making a valid point about the market research that goes on in businesses, most people would accept that such research is vital for market-orientated firms. As such, any decision to cut research activity is clearly short-sighted and not likely to be in the firm's long-term interest. The quote, perhaps, says more about the ability of the firm to analyse and use its data than it does about the quantity of information gathered.

A small manufacturing firm does not have its own market research function. Instead, it relies heavily on secondary data. Assess the likely impact such a strategy might have for the firm.

(40 marks)

Any assessment of a business strategy requires a consideration of both the benefits and disadvantages for the firm, so that a considered conclusion can be drawn. Better answers will be made relevant to the specific situation described in the question. In this case, the answer ought to consider a manufacturing firm. Note that the question uses the phrase 'relies heavily'. This implies that some primary research is also used, so it would be a mistake to write about a firm which *only* used secondary data.

Points in favour of such a strategy that could be developed are:

■ It is cheaper to use secondary data than to undertake a lot of primary research.

■ The firm may manufacture exclusively for a retailer and, as such, its production may be largely dictated by the retailer.

■ If the firm is in a traditional market which tends to change slowly, if at all, then the use of secondary data may be satisfactory.

On the other hand:

■ It can be argued that all markets change over time, and that in most cases the rate of change is increasing. Only by undertaking appropriate primary research can the firm be fully aware of the changes it faces in its marketplace.

■ Even manufacturing firms need to be consumer orientated – a reliance on secondary data could distort the firm's view of the marketplace.

In conclusion, it is likely that a firm which relies too heavily on secondary data may be putting itself at a competitive disadvantage – other firms may be able to spot opportunities or threats before this firm, react quicker to them and will be more prepared to cope with change. Only in very rare cases is this strategy likely to be one that leads to long-term success.

To what extent is sampling a useful method of market research?

(40 marks)

As with all essay type questions, there are clearly two aspects to this one. However, it is not as simple as looking at the benefits and drawbacks of sampling. By definition, sampling produces problems rather than giving much in the way of direct benefits. In this question, the potential negative effects of sampling can be balanced against a discussion of the reasons why the issues are not as negative as they may appear.

The potential negative effects could be:

■ inaccuracy

■ uncertainty.

On the other hand students could argue that:

■ statistical techniques exist to ensure a high degree of accuracy

■ sampling findings will not be used in isolation, but with other data, intuition and experience.

In conclusion, the use of sampling is inevitable in market research, due to the cost and impracticality of testing a whole population. The key lies not in the sampling itself, but in how the data is collected, analysed and interpreted.

'Small firms should spend a larger proportion of their resources on market research than large firms.' Evaluate this statement.

(40 marks)

No matter what the size of a firm, the importance of consumer orientation holds true. The proportion of resources to be spent on market research will, of course, vary from firm to firm, and from one situation to the next. To evaluate this statement, then, requires an awareness of the factors influencing the amount of market research to be undertaken. These factors can then be applied to the differences likely to exist between large and small firms. Note that the question talks about the proportion of spending, not the total amounts. Large firms will almost always spend more on market research, but may not always spend a larger proportion of their resources.

Some possible factors to consider could be:

■ *The scope of the business* – large firms tend to operate in many markets, in terms of both products, services and geographical location. Each market has to be researched. It may be, then, that such a firm needs to spend a greater proportion of its resources on research than a smaller firm operating in a single, localised and familiar market.

■ *Analytical ability* – smaller firms may not have sufficient expertise or time to make the gathering of research data an effective use of its limited resources. If larger firms can make better use of research data, it follows that they will spend comparatively more on its collection.

On the other hand:

■ *Vulnerability* – since smaller firms are more at risk from slight changes in the marketplace than larger ones, it follows that they ought to keep a closer watch on developments if they are to survive in their competitive environment. There is, then, a greater need for smaller firms to put more resources into market research.

■ *Niche markets* – smaller firms often survive and prosper in niche markets. By definition, though, niche markets are more likely to experience rapid changes than mass markets. Again, the implication is that smaller firms operating in niche markets are the ones that most need the assistance of research data.

It would appear that the statement is more likely to be true, but it does not take into account the practical difficulties involved in putting the strategy into practice. Although the need exists for small firms to spend a greater proportion of their resources on market research, the ability may not justify this spending.

Student answers

Discuss the possible implications for a company's marketing decisions of holding detailed data on their customers.

(11 marks)

Student answer

Detailed data will help the firm to make better marketing decisions, so that the firm will be able to sell more and make more profit. By knowing a person's buying habits, for example, the firm will be able to produce adverts that appeal to them. Customers will buy the firm's products instead of rivals, and they will become more successful.

Marker's comments

This answer contains the germ of a good idea, and the candidate goes some way to using that idea to explain a possible consequence. Unfortunately, the idea is not fully explored, and the language used is rather too extreme. Also the link between targeting customers and increasing profits is too superficial here, with no consideration of the other links in the chain.

A better answer would have taken a broader perspective – if one firm has very detailed data, so might its competitors.

The answer attracts one mark for raising a relevant idea, and some more for its simplistic application of the idea in the answer, but scores nothing for depth of analysis or evaluation.

Mark: Content 1/2, Application & Analysis 3/6, Evaluation 0/3. Total = 4

Consider whether the use of sampling detracts from the value of market research.

(11 marks)

Student answer

The use of sampling is necessary because of the difficulty and cost of questioning everyone in the market. Therefore, market research using samples can not be 100% accurate. However, if a large representative sample is used, then the answers can be used with a high degree of confidence. Also, if managers are to make the best decisions they will not rely just on the market research data. They will also use other information, their own past experience and their judgement. So while a 100% sample would give perfect data, small samples can still give a good basis for making decisions.

Marker's comments

It is clear from this answer that the writer has a good knowledge of the issues surrounding the question. There is a clear attempt to give both sides of the argument and to arrive at a conclusion based on these arguments. Although the key issues are raised, they are dealt with very briefly and not explored in any depth. The conclusion, though, is a valid one. A stronger answer may have returned to the idea of sampling 'detracting' from the value of research.

Mark: Content 2/2, Application & Analysis 4/6, Evaluation 1/2. Total = 7

Discuss the ways in which recent developments in Information Technology have improved the ability of firms to carry out effective market research.

(11 marks)

Student answer

Recent developments in IT have given firms two main benefits for carrying out effective market research. Firstly, it has meant that it is quicker to collect data through such systems as EPOS and easier to store data from researchers. Both of these mean that the firm has a lot of up-to-date information from which to make its marketing decisions. By making the firm's response time quicker, it is more likely to be able to meet the needs of consumers when they are still current.

Secondly, the developments in IT have allowed firms to process more data more accurately. This again ought to make firms more able to make accurate marketing decisions.

Altogether, the developments in IT ought to make a firm's decisions better. However, it must be remembered that other firms in the same market are likely to have the same facilities, and so these improvements are not likely to give the firm any great competitive advantage.

Marker's comments

This is a well structured answer that clearly sets out some useful points. The second point could have been developed further to good effect. The final paragraph shows a broad appreciation of the wider context of business and clearly sets the question into a broader context. The final idea that other firms may also be developing their IT systems is a good point.

Mark: Content 2/2, Application & Analysis 5/6, Evaluation 2/3. Total = 9

"More data leads to better decisions.' Discuss.

(11 marks)

Student answer

It seems obvious that more data will lead to better decisions for a business, but this is not always the case. There could be information overload, which leads to managers not being able to see the wood for the trees. There is a danger that managers will not notice the really important pieces of data in time and so the decisions that they make will be the wrong ones.

It can be said that more information actually leads to worse decisions in the long run, not better ones.

Marker's comments

Any discussion requires two sides, but unfortunately this answer is very limited in its scope, offering a single perspective. Not only are the advantages of more information overlooked, the discussion that is present is grossly overstated and lacks a true perspective. The underlying idea is interesting but not explored in any depth.

Mark: Content 1/2, Application & Analysis 3/6, Evaluation 0/3. Total = 4

End of section questions

1 Discuss the possible value of market research in determining a firm's strategy.

(11 marks)

2 Examine the value of secondary data.

(9 marks)

3 Examine the possible limitations of using samples in the collection of research data.

(9 marks)

4 To what extent can firms undertake too much market research?

(11 marks)

5 How might a firm decide on the level of its market research spending?

(9 marks)

6 To what extent should market research be considered a science?

(11 marks)

7 Analyse the contribution that market research can make to the success of a firm.

(9 marks)

8 Is a hunch a better way of making a decision than using market research?

(11 marks)

9 Evaluate the usefulness of historically-based data on decisions about the future.

(11 marks)

10 To what extent have developments in information technology improved market research?

(11 marks)

Essays

1 'Market research is often wrong so why bother with it?' Discuss.

(40 marks)

2 Assess the view that secondary data is more useful to a firm than primary data.

(40 marks)

3 'Market research is useful for existing products, but can tell us relatively little about innovative ones.' How far do you agree with this statement?

(40 marks)

4 'We are market leaders. Other firms follow our innovations. Why should we use our resources on market research?' Justify the spending to this chief executive.

(40 marks)

5 A firm is facing financial difficulties, largely due to a falling market share. Should the firm increase or decrease its spending on market research? Justify your answer.

(40 marks)

Marketing audit

Introduction

A marketing audit is the process of assessing a firm's marketing performance, just as a financial audit considers the financial performance of the firm. The scope of the marketing audit, however, is broader, taking into account both the *internal* factors and the aspects of the *external* environment which may impact on the firm's performance. For some firms, the marketing audit is part of the budgetary process, acting as a check on how the money allocated to the marketing department is being used, whilst for others it forms a central strand of the marketing strategic decision-making process.

The SWOT

One possible format for a marketing audit is the SWOT model (Strengths, Weaknesses, Opportunities and Threats, see page 27). Using this technique the firm can assess:

- its marketing strengths, such as being market leader or having extensive distribution networks

- its marketing weaknesses, such as having products that are losing share to competitors or ones with a poor public image

- its marketing opportunities; these are the areas where it has the chance to improve its marketing performance, such as a new niche or a brand name that can be extended

- its marketing threats, where competitors appear to be gaining at the firm's expense, of where existing products are no longer performing as well as they had done previously.

The data generated by SWOT-type analyses can act as a guide to a firm in its decision-making. It may decide to build on its strengths, or regard the elimination of weaknesses as the main priority. Alternatively, it may decide to exploit the opportunities revealed or try to counter the threats it faces. Since the firm is unlikely to have the resources to tackle fully all of these areas, it must attempt to balance its marketing spending to gain the best overall effect.

> **The marketing audit identifies the existing position of the firm so that it can plan effectively.**

FACT FILE

The UK consumer's appetite for crisps, nuts and other savoury snacks is increasing rapidly. In 1998, for example, the average consumer ate almost 7 kg of snacks! The market is now worth well over £2 bn, up over £500 m since 1994. This is compared with flat sales of milk and an increase of about 1.6% for bread and rolls. The reason for this growth is an increase in grazing by consumers (eating less more often). The market is expected to be worth nearly £2.9 bn by 2003. The fastest growth will be in cereal bars such as Kellogg's Nutrigrain and Rice Krispie Squares. One of the biggest successes of recent years has been Procter and Gamble's Pringles crisps which have taken 6% of the crisp market despite being more expensive.

Source: Financial Times 22 September 1999

A full marketing audit can be costly, although the information from which it is compiled is usually coming into the business at various times for other purposes, such as market research and sales analysis. The larger the firm, the more likely it is that frequent audits will be undertaken. Small firms are likely to have less need for a formal process of market audit, especially if they are single product/service firms operating in a single market. The larger the firm and the more diverse its operations, the greater the need for a comprehensive review of the firm's marketing situation in the form of an audit.

> **PROGRESS CHECK**
>
> Explain the possible reasons for undertaking a marketing audit.

Specific tools of analysis

Portfolio analysis

During a marketing audit, a firm can use some specific tools of analysis to establish its marketing situation. Each contributes to the whole picture of the firm's situation. Amongst these techniques is the concept of **portfolio analysis**, which helps to identify the position of each of the firm's products within their market. Portfolio analysis includes the notion of the **product life cycle** (see page 75), which examines the sales of a 'typical' product (if such a thing exists) at different stages of its life, and the idea of **market segmentation** (see page 78), which can lead to the identification of new markets for existing or newly developed products.

> **PROGRESS CHECK**
>
> ## Questions
>
> 1 Why is it important for a firm to undertake a marketing audit?
> 2 Consider how the results of a marketing audit might be used.

The Boston Matrix

One of the most famous methods of portfolio analysis was developed by the Boston Consulting Group and is known as the **Boston Matrix** (or Boston Box).

This method of portfolio analysis examines the position of a firm's products in terms of their relative market share and market growth. The Boston Matrix is illustrated in figure 5.1.

Using this model a firm can quickly assess the position of its products in their relative markets, and from this make a decision as to how the product ought to be treated in the future. The labels used are deliberately humourous and help people to remember the model, as well as indicating the state of the product. Each circle represents the position of a product (or business if the firm is evaluating the position of its different business units); the area of the circle represents the product's turnover. The four types of products are described below:

1 As a rough guide, the products on which the future of the firm depends are the **Stars** – not only do they have a strong position in their market, but the market

Market share

High   Low

High   Star   Problem child

Market growth

Low   Cash cow   Dog

Figure 5.1 The Boston Matrix

itself is growing, suggesting that the sales potential of this product type is high. It, therefore, follows that marketing resources and effort ought to be channelled into developing and supporting these products.

2 **Problem Children** are the products with potential which has yet to be realised. Their market is growing, but at the moment these products only account for a small market share. If the firm is willing and able to put its resources behind these products, it may be rewarded. These products are likely to turn into the 'Stars' of the future by taking a larger share of their markets.

3 **Cash Cows** have a large market share in slow growing markets; they are likely to remain solid earners without the need for a great deal of investment. In time, as growing markets reach their limits and settle down into a more stable position, today's Stars become the Cash Cows of tomorrow. They often provide the finance for the development of future 'Stars'.

4 **Dogs** are, in many ways, the 'no-hopers' of the firm's product portfolio. They play a small part in a market that is barely developing, if at all. There may be sound business reasons for keeping hold of 'dogs'. They might, for example, complete a product range, but in broad financial and marketing terms they are contributing little to the firm and may well be dropped.

A product portfolio will ideally be balanced between the different types of products shown in the Boston Matrix. Cash Cows are needed to fund any investment in Problem Children, while 'Stars' could not support themselves in the long term.

FACT FILE

Unfortunately for businesses, Dogs tend to outweigh Stars. One estimate suggested that in the USA, the proportion of business units in each category were: 72% Dogs; 15% Cash Cows; 10% Problem Children; 3% Stars.

PROGRESS CHECK

Questions

1 Undertake some research into the range of products of a large, multi-product firm such as Diageo. Place each product into the appropriate section of the Boston Matrix.

2 Examine how the Boston Matrix can help a firm with its marketing planning.

How useful is the Boston Matrix?

As an aid to decision-making, the Boston Matrix is quick, easy to use and allows generalised decisions to be made very quickly. As such, it is a fair starting point for decision-making. However, it also has some limitations. The model is based on two assumptions that do not always hold:

1 *'The success of a product can be measured by its market share.'* This may be true in some markets, but in many consumer product markets a market share of 5–10% is considered a good performance. There are other measures of success which may be a better guide to the future potential of the product, such as the attitude of consumers to the product or the product's quality. In many cases the measure of success will be determined by the objective of the business. From another perspective, a large market share does not necessarily reflect a good product. A current high share may be a mask for complacency and hide the fact that the product is no longer developing to meet changing consumer demand; a Star may be faced with a rapid demotion to Cash Cow or Dog status.

2 *'A fast growing market is the best place to be.'* Whilst there are advantages to being part of a fast growing market, there are serious drawbacks as well. The rate of growth may attract heavy competition, and, if the number of competitors becomes too large, these products may require price reductions leading to falling profit margins. A high rate of growth could encourage a firm to invest heavily in a particular area for the future, only to find that the rate of growth suddenly slows leaving the firm with a great deal of underused capacity.

As with all such techniques there is a danger if the model is taken too literally. Any decision should be based on much more than this simple model. A firm which aims to be particularly innovative, for example, may want more Stars than a conservative business. A firm operating in a fast changing market may be concerned about having too many Cash Cows and not enough potential new products, compared to a business producing in a slow moving market.

The Boston Matrix, in itself, is simply a diagram illustrating the *existing* position of the firms' products. This can help to highlight a particular position but it does not actually make any decisions – decisions need the skill, experience, vision and ability of the management. Good managers make the right decisions more times than they make the wrong ones; bad managers will not. How many people would have decided to revive Lucozade, Horlicks or Tango, for example? It may have been much easier to get rid of them.

PROGRESS CHECK

Analyse the possible value of the Boston Matrix model for marketing decision-making.

The product life cycle

The product life cycle is a graph that illustrates the sales level of a product or brand over time. The idea is that, just as humans move through several stages in life, products also develop according to a certain pattern. The general pattern of sales is shown in figure 5.2.

Initially, sales grow slowly when a product is launched. Following this, there is often a fairly steep rise as the product becomes known and is adopted by consumers. Eventually, sales reach a stable level, where they remain until the product is overtaken by new developments or changing tastes, at which time the product may die. By recognising the distinct stage that a product has reached, a firm can decide how to treat it in marketing terms.

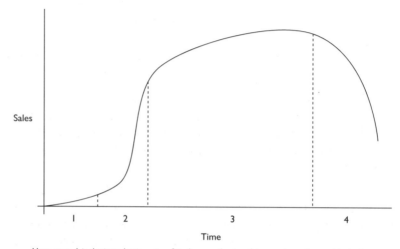

Here, stage 1 is the introduction, stage 2 is the growth, stage 3 is maturity and stage 4 is decline.

Figure 5.2 A generalised product life cycle

A common misconception is that the product life cycle can be used to predict what is going to happen to a product in the future. In reality, the concept is highly generalised. Knowing that a product's sales are growing is possibly (but not certainly) an indication that the product is in its growth stage. This does not tell the firm anything about how long this stage is going to last or how high the growth will be, although market research may give some clues above this. Similarly the length of the maturity phase can vary enormously from one product to the next.

PROGRESS CHECK

Identify a product in each stage of the product life cycle. For each, explain why you think it is at that stage.

How useful is the product life cycle?

Although the product life cycle is of very limited use as a forecasting tool, its real strength lies in its use as a means of planning and of control. The concept goes on to characterise the main marketing features of each stage of the product's life and suggests certain marketing strategies that may be appropriate. It also allows the performance of current products to be compared with similar ones at the same life cycle stage in the past, to gauge how well the product is doing.

Life cycle marketing strategies

Potential strategies for each stage of the life cycle are:

- Introduction: during this stage the strategy to be followed very much depends on the type of product and its market. The firm could decide to attempt a high profile launch to produce rapid acceptance before competitors launch similar products. Such a strategy would mean a high spend on promotions, together with a high price. A low profile launch may be appropriate if consumers are already aware of the product or if the market is price elastic.

- *Growth*: the aim for the firm here is to prolong the growth in sales for as long as possible, by enhancing the product's competitive position. Possible ways of achieving this are through improving product quality and features, finding new market segments or reducing the price to encourage a greater take up of the product.

- *Maturity*: this is the most common state for products and most marketing strategies can be applied. The aim is to maintain the maturity stage as long as possible, perhaps even moving it to a higher level through product developments or finding new markets. Any element of the marketing mix can be changed to enhance the product and retain its market position.

- *Decline*: once a product is in decline, a firm has three alternatives. It can keep things as they are until the product is no longer feasible, it can drop the product immediately from its portfolio or it can 'milk' the product by halting marketing spending on the product and allowing it to continue to sell at an increased profit margin.

As a marketing tool, the product life cycle, like the Boston Matrix, is at best a starting point for the decision-making process. It is very difficult to identify with certainty the point a product has reached in its life cycle at any given time and, even if this is known, it says little about what the future holds for the product. The generalised model may help to explain past events, but really only gives a broad framework within which to make decisions on marketing strategies to suit the product's needs.

There is a real danger that the life cycle model becomes self-fulfilling. Believing that products enter the growth phase after they are launched may encourage firms to put resources into promotion and distribution which then help to bring about such growth. Believing that decline is inevitable may cause firms to cut back on their marketing activities, therefore bringing about the fall in sales which was initially expected.

PROGRESS CHECK

How useful is the product life cycle model?

Is the decline of a product inevitable?

In many cases the decline in sales of a product is brought about by poor marketing. Managers may fail to identify changes in the market, perhaps not appreciating the impact of competition or not adapting the product appropriately. The continued success of brands such as Coca Cola, Kellogg's Cornflakes and Barbie dolls shows that decline can be staved off by effective marketing – new designs, new packaging, new sizes, new varieties, new markets and new distribution channels have kept these products very successful.

Having said this, markets can suddenly disappear or fall in value due to external factors. Decline is then all but inevitable – the rise of the wordprocessor has considerably reduced the typewriter market; market trends in the UK have made various high fat foods difficult to sell. On the other hand, despite adverse publicity, severe taxation policies and aggressive legislation to reduce consumption, the continued success of tobacco products shows what can be achieved through marketing (although continued sales are also likely to be due to the addictive nature of the product). The ongoing sales of products such as Fairy Liquid, Ariel, Oxo and Bic biros shows how effective marketing can postpone the decline phase of the life cycle. However, in order to achieve results like this, managers must pay continual attention to their marketing activities, updating and reviewing.

PROGRESS CHECK

Is the decline stage of the product life cycle inevitable?

Market segmentation

Rather than look at a marketplace as a single entity, market segmentation attempts to break the whole market down into smaller groups that share common characteristics. This helps firms in two ways. Firstly, firms can see if their existing products may be suitable for a new market segment and, secondly, they can consider whether an unexploited market segment could be addressed through the development of a new or amended product from their portfolio.

The arguments in favour of market segmentation can be summarised as follows:

- By targeting small groups, a firm can respond effectively to individual (or small group) needs, thereby placing the consumer at the centre of its marketing strategy.

- Competitive advantage can be gained by fulfilling the specialised needs of groups of customers.

- Resources are likely to be used more efficiently if they are targeted more precisely.

- By responding to new opportunities, the firm is taking advantage of its changing environment.

There are, however, counter arguments to using market segmentation, such as:

- Segmentation implies shorter production runs which may cause unit costs to rise as a consequence.

- There is a greater reliance on market research data as a basis for decision-making, even when there may be limitations with such data (see Chapter 4).

- There is likely to be higher costs for stock holding and administration.

The core debate about market segmentation centres on the financial implications of being able to respond to the needs of consumers. Modern production methods, with their emphasis on short production runs and flexibility, tend to make market segmentation more feasible for production companies. Many people would argue that modern marketing and production systems rely on market segmentation to keep a competitive advantage.

FACT FILE

Land Rover vehicles are available in a variety of styles and colours with a range of accessories as extras. In the past, a customer may have had to wait weeks or even months to get the exact vehicle they wanted. With today's flexible production methods, a specific order can be delivered within two working days.

PROGRESS CHECK

Examine the possible benefits of market segmentation.

To what extent is segmentation useful?

This depends on whether the segments in the market are easy to identify and whether the likely long-term returns make it worth entering a market segment. The firm must also be able to meet the needs of the customers within the segments which have been identified, and be able to protect itself against future competition. The benefits of segmentation must be weighed up against the cost disadvantages of small production runs and the greater complexity of managing a multi-product firm. In some industries and for some firms, the use of flexible production techniques (such as lean production) has made segmentation more attractive. At the same time, there has been a move towards standardising as much as possible of the production process and simply adapting particular features to market requirements. This is known as **mass customisation**. The basic design of a Electrolux fridge, for example, is fairly standard but the layout of the different sections inside can be adapted to customer requirements.

KEY POINTS

Market segmentation is more useful if:

- the segments are clearly identifiable
- the segments are profitable and sustainable
- the firm can meet the demands of the segments
- the firm can exploit its USPs
- the unit cost disadvantages are not significant
- the firm has a flexible production process.

PROGRESS CHECK

Consider the possible disadvantages to a firm of market segmentation.

Conclusion

Marketing audits form a valuable basis from which marketing decisions can be made. Some specific analytical tools can be used to determine a marketing strategy for each of the products in a firm's portfolio. However, the marketing audit does not provide the firm with any *answers*. It provides some specialised information about the current situation facing the firm and about what has happened in the past. The art of the marketing strategist is to take this current and historical data, blend it with the objectives of the firm, other internal information and experience, to arrive at a conclusion which will help the firm to achieve its targets. However,

KEY TERM

USP, or unique selling point (or proposition) is the thing that differentiates one product or service from the next. It gives the firm a competitive advantage.

the *process* of auditing is useful in itself – it forces firms to question their existing products, methods and performance and to consider the value of their marketing activities.

> **A marketing audit helps provide managers with the information they need. It does not guarantee success.**

Summary chart

Figure 5.3 Key elements of marketing audits

Approaching exam questions: Marketing audit

'The product life cycle is more likely to be seen in the classroom than the boardroom.' Assess the implications of this statement for marketing managers.

(40 marks)

In essence, this question is asking the student to demonstrate both the usefulness and limitations of business theory in the real world of business management. The two sides of the answer, then, will cover these two aspects before arriving at a reasoned conclusion which emphasises the impact of this particular theory for the type of managers specified.

The usefulness of the theory may be explained by reference to these points:

■ The model gives a framework through which changes in a product's fortunes can be explained.

■ It allows managers to devise appropriate strategies for a product's circumstances.

■ The performance of a product can be judged against previous products at a similar stage of the life cycle.

The limitations of the theory could be highlighted through discussion of:

■ the difficulties of determining a product's current position

■ the impossibility of using the model to predict what will happen next in the product's life

■ the problems of spotting the change-over points from one sector to another.

In conclusion, the theory has its uses but by no means provides answers for marketing managers. The theory must be taken alongside all other available information before a valid judgement can be made about the 'best' strategy for developing the competitive advantages of each particular product.

Analyse the impact on marketing of moving from a mass market approach to a market segmentation approach for a producer of consumer durables.

(9 marks)

The positive impacts could include the fact that the firm will be:

■ more responsive to changes in consumer demand

■ more adaptable to changing circumstances

- more cost efficient as spending is more tightly focused.

On the negative side, impacts could be:

- a higher unit cost, possibly necessitating an increase in price and, therefore, difficulties in selling
- less certainty, making long-term planning more difficult
- an increase in the costs and difficulties of communication, which must become much more efficient to cope with market segmentation.

In conclusion, the type of firm and its particular circumstances will determine whether or not the move will have an overall beneficial effect. If the firm is large, can afford to adopt flexible production methods, has strong communication links and a culture that accepts change, then it is likely to benefit from the move. Small firms with a limited presence in the market may find it very difficult to cope with all the implications of such a move.

Evaluate the strategies available for a producer of fast moving consumer goods who finds all its Star products are becoming Cash Cows.

(40 marks)

An essay question that contains some specialised jargon such as this one would benefit from some brief definitions, before moving on to address the actual question set. In this case, the writer must be clear about what makes a product a Star or a Cash Cow.

The phrasing of this question indicates that the writer should highlight at least two possible strategies. Three possible strategies are given below.

1 If all its Stars are becoming Cash Cows, the firm will be provided with a solid income flow for the foreseeable future. This flow could be used to promote any Problem Children to the status of Stars through a strong, high-profile marketing campaign. The benefits of such a strategy include the possibility of producing high returns from new Stars, a problem might be the possibility of failure.
2 The firm could look to develop new markets or new uses for its existing Stars to prevent the move to Cash Cows from happening. Such a strategy is likely to be costly, but would give long-term rewards, especially benefiting the product's brand name.
3 The financing from the Cash Cows could be used to develop entirely new products, aimed at undeveloped market segments. This would allow the development of a new group of Stars. The possibility of failure and the timescale involved would have to be set against the expected returns.

In conclusion, however, it could be noted that the changes being described are unlikely to be happening in the short term. Why has the firm not noticed the movement before and taken appropriate action to balance its portfolio before now? The case highlights the need for firms to keep a sharp watch on their product portfolio at all times.

Evaluate the contribution that marketing audits can make to business success.

(11 marks)

A single factor, such as marketing audits, can make only a limited contribution to something as general as 'business success'. Any evaluation, then, will need to consider both the contribution that can be made and the limitations to that contribution.

The contribution could include:

- Marketing audits allow a firm to keep a check on the performance of all its products, so that it does not face problems caused by unanticipated change.

- It allows firms to become consumer-orientated – products are constantly being appraised against the state of their market and their performance in it.

However, the limitations of marketing audits are:

- The models used are only a simplistic representation of the marketplace and so cannot be relied upon to present an accurate picture.

- The success of any business relies on the integration of all the business's functions, so the contribution of each one is necessarily limited.

In conclusion, marketing audits are important to business success, but the technique cannot guarantee success. Audits are, therefore, necessary but not sufficient for business success.

Student answers

Analyse the possible benefits of a marketing audit.

(9 marks)

Student answer

A marketing audit involves an examination of the existing position of a firm. This is important as part of the planning process – if you do not know where you are, you cannot plan effectively. The process of the audit involves discussion and forces managers to consider the existing strengths and weaknesses of the firm. Having identified these, the firm can exploit its strengths and/or defend itself against its weaknesses. For example, it may extend its brand or develop a new product to fill a gap in the market. Firms which do not undertake an audit are likely to take greater risks in their planning, because the plan may bear little resemblance to the firm's abilities or resources. However, the benefits of the audit must be weighed up against the costs and time involved in the process.

Marker's comments

This is quite a good answer which clearly highlights the value of the process in planning as well as pointing out the dangers of not undertaking an audit.

Mark: Content 2/2, Application 4/4, Analysis 1/3. Total = 7

Analyse the value of segmentation to a firm.

(9 marks)

Student answer

By segmenting a market, a firm can clearly identify the different needs of customer groups. This can be done by age, gender, income, usage pattern, region and so on. This means the firm learns more about its customers, their buying habits and what they think. This can be very useful indeed. The more you know the better it is.

Marker's comments

This is a weak answer which makes assertions but does not develop or defend these. Why is segmentation useful? How does it help firms? What can they do with the additional information?

Mark: Content 2/2, Application 0/4, Analysis 0/3. Total = 2

End of section questions

1 Examine the circumstances in which it may be appropriate for a firm to sustain the production of Dogs.

(9 marks)

2 Examine the ways in which the book market might be segmented and the implication of this for a firm's marketing.

(9 marks)

3 Examine the circumstances in which a product may avoid the decline stage of the product life cycle.

(9 marks)

4 Assess the usefulness of a SWOT analysis to a firm's marketing planning.

(11 marks)

5 To what extent is the product life cycle model essential to the marketing planning process?

(11 marks)

6 Assess the value of the Boston Matrix for marketing planning.

(11 marks)

7 Analysis the importance of niche marketing in the modern business environment.

(11 marks)

8 Examine the role of portfolio analysis in marketing planning.

(9 marks)

9 Is a marketing audit essential to a firm?

(11 marks)

10 Analyse the possible implications for a firm of not undertaking marketing audits.

(9 marks)

Essays

1 'Firms which do not undertake a marketing audit are bound to fail.' Discuss.

(40 marks)

2 To what extent does undertaking a marketing audit ensure that a firm will develop a successful marketing strategy?

(40 marks)

3 'The Boston Matrix is an interesting model but of no practical value.' Discuss.

(40 marks)

4 'Good marketers know what to do intuitively – they do not need to undertake a marketing audit.' Discuss.

(40 marks)

5 'The product life cycle model is self-fulfilling.' Critically assess this view.

(40 marks)

The marketing mix

Introduction

The four Ps

The marketing mix is one of the central concepts in the study of marketing. In the form first proposed by McCarthy in the 1950s, the marketing mix consists of **four P's** – **P**roduct, **P**romotion, **P**lacing and **P**ricing. Like so many ideas that catch the imagination, the concept appears a simple one, and yet it hides considerable depth and insight. The four Ps briefly describe the basic marketing decisions that need to be taken in order to produce a coherent marketing strategy. To be successful, the elements of the marketing mix must be integrated and should complement each other.

> **The marketing mix consists of all the aspects of a product or service which contribute to its appeal to customers.**

Unfortunately, the simplicity that gives rise to much of the appeal of the four Ps model has also caused some marketing analysts to feel that the model is limited. In restricting the development of a marketing strategy to four basic features, it has been argued that other key factors have been missed. For example, improvements in the technology associated with packaging has led to many writers suggesting that packaging is a fifth 'P', although others do try to include it as part of 'promotion' within the four Ps. Other commentators suggest that a major component of a firm's marketing activities is the people in the organisation who do the marketing function. More fundamentally, a key component of any marketing decision is marketing intelligence – the information gathered from market research and audits.

PROGRESS CHECK

How can the marketing mix support the achievement of the firm's strategic aims?

More Ps and other factors

Packaging

Up to the 1930s, many goods were sold without any form of packaging. Commodities such as bread and meat were on open display in shops and were wrapped in plain paper after purchase. Today, supermarket shelves are filled with bright, colourful and enticing packages and, in many cases, the actual product cannot be seen at all. Clearly, this packaging forms part of the promotional function for the product. However, the packaging used today does more than attract customers to pick products off the shelves. In many cases the packaging has become an integral part of the product. Drinks in cans have replaced the need for glasses and the cans have been redesigned in recent years to be safer, more reliable and now, with larger openings, more convenient to use. Some products can be cooked in the microwave in their original packaging. Under development at the moment is a square food can with flexible walls. The product is small for ease of transport and storage, but when the product (the can and its contents) is cooked, the flexibility allows the product to expand to the size of normal portions.

The packaging industry in the UK is estimated to have a value of £10 bn per year. As well as encouraging the customer to pick up the product from the supermarket shelves, packaging can add to the performance and convenience of the product. As such, it can give a product a competitive advantage over a similar product that lacks the additional features given by the package. It is for this reason that some writers feel that packaging is more than a part of the promotional aspect of the four Ps and ought to be considered as a separate part of the development of a marketing strategy.

Questions   PROGRESS CHECK

1 Explain how the packaging of a product may influence its success in the market place.
2 How important is packaging in the marketing mix?

Processes

Processes refers to the experience of the consumer in acquiring a product. As a part of the marketing mix, a firm needs to ensure that its products can be bought with relative ease. This is particularly true with 'mid-range' items. Fast moving consumer goods, commonly bought by consumers, can be purchased easily at many retail outlets. High price, infrequently bought items, such as cars, washing machines or houses may have a more complex buying process. Official documents need to be available for inspection, extra insurance considered, possibly credit agreements arranged and signed. Because such transactions happen rarely for an individual, a relatively complex buying process is acceptable. However, consumers are likely to be put off buying mid-range goods, such as mobile phones, designer clothes or computer games, if the buying process involves such a degree of complexity. So, as part of the marketing mix, a firm must ensure that potential customers can acquire the product with relative ease, perhaps by offering scope for buying over the phone, by reducing the number of forms to fill in, if any, or by arranging payment by credit card, as well as by cash or cheque.

PROGRESS CHECK

Explain how the following types of firms might change the buying process to gain a competitive advantage:

- retailers
- banks
- restaurants.

People

All workers are marketers

One phrase that is associated with Japanese production methods is that 'all workers are marketers'; every action undertaken by every employee in the firm impacts on how well the firm meets the needs of its customers and, therefore, on its marketing position as well. This applies clearly to the case of service industries where workers often come into direct contact with the customer. It equally applies, though, to manufacturing industries where the quality of work from the whole staff influences the quality of the final output.

Quality is free

A production idea that is spreading through modern businesses is equally applicable to marketing. Crosby is credited with the idea that 'quality is free'. This refers to the cost savings that are made by getting everything right first time. If there is no need to re-work a product or scrap it because of problems in its manufacture, the firm wastes less, and saves money and resources. As a marketing tool, getting everything right first time allows the firm to develop a competitive advantage, perhaps through the quality and reliability of the product or through a cheaper selling price. However, making sure that everything is done properly first time requires a massive culture shift for most businesses in the UK. Traditionally, workers produced a good and someone else further down the production line checked the quality, and scrapped or sent back defective items. Quality rested with the inspectors, not the workers. The adoption by workers of the responsibility for quality places them directly into the marketing mix.

> **Everyone in a firm has a customer (whether internal or external). Everyone in a firm is involved in marketing.**

PROGRESS CHECK

'People are a key element of a firm's marketing mix.' Discuss.

Marketing intelligence

A common definition of the marketing mix is 'the factors a firm needs to consider to develop an effective marketing strategy'. As shown in Chapters 1 and 2 an effective marketing strategy is one that addresses the needs and wants of consumers. Consumer orientation requires that a firm places the consumer at the heart of all its marketing decisions. This being the case, the traditional marketing mix of the four Ps is clearly inadequate. A firm could make decisions on each of the four traditional elements without regard for the needs of the consumer. If such a firm was in a competitive market, it is likely that it would lose out to rivals who were meeting more closely the needs of customers. It is argued that the four Ps alone are insufficient to produce an effective marketing strategy. By adding marketing intelligence into the mix, a firm is more likely to be able to produce a marketing strategy that fulfils its primary aim of meeting the needs of consumers.

FACT FILE

Captain Kirk in *Star Trek* never said 'Beam me up, Scotty'. Sherlock Holmes in Conan Doyle's stories never said 'Elementary, my dear Watson'. Humphrey Bogart in *Casablanca* never said 'Play it again, Sam'.
Marketing decisions are never made on the basis of the four Ps alone!

> **Marketing intelligence provides firms with the information they need to make better decisions.**

PROGRESS CHECK

Outline the possible contribution of packaging, processes and marketing intelligence to the traditional marketing mix in relation to the following products or services:

- soft drinks
- clothes
- computer equipment.

FACT FILE

In 1998, researchers asked 1000 children aged between 3 and 12 years from Britain, Italy, France and Germany what they most wanted. For British children clothes topped the list of presents by 25.5%; next was a bike (16.7%); then sweets (13.8%); books (12%) and a TV (11.3%). The 1997 'must-have' present, a Teletubby, was 88th.

Figure 6.1 An extended marketing mix

Firms with effective marketing intelligence are more likely to succeed because:

- they have a better understanding of the market
- they are more aware of competitors' actions
- they are more aware of the different options open to them
- they can monitor the success of their plans more successfully.

What determines the 'right' marketing mix?

The marketing mix can never be static. The market in which a product is sold, like the whole of the business environment, is dynamic.

Successful marketing must be adapted to meet changing circumstances.

Some of the key variables that should be considered when determining the marketing mix are shown in table 6.1. In addition to these factors are two fundamental elements that ought to underpin all marketing mix decisions. These are the market in which the product is being sold and the stage reached in the product's life cycle.

FACTOR	EXAMPLE
Type of product	If the firm produces consumer goods, price or packaging may be emphasised. Luxury goods may rely more on image and product quality.
Degree of competition	In a competitive market, a firm might stress distribution and price, or may attempt to differentiate its products.
The position of the business in the market	Market leaders have more flexibility in their mix than followers, who often follow the trends in the marketplace.
Changes in the marketing mix of competitors	Firms have to be constantly aware of the marketing actions of competitors in the market. If one gives a price discount, should the move be followed, or should advertising be increased?

Table 6.1 Factors influencing the marketing mix

> **The marketing mix should not be fixed – it is a set of tools which should be adjusted regularly to meet new challenges. Success requires the right tools for the job.**

How do marketing mixes differ?

The marketing mix differs in different markets. Certain aspects of the mix may be common to firms in the same industry.

Industrial markets

In this type of market one firm may be producing machinery, components etc. and selling them to other firms where they are used in the manufacture of other products. The specifications of the product are usually agreed between the buyer and seller, to meet the specific needs of the buyer. This gives the producer little control over the product life cycle. If the producer is to keep the contract to supply the buyer, it has to prove that the product can meet the agreed specifications, is of a suitable quality and is supplied on time.

The role of the salesforce is often critical in the marketing of industrial products; the salesforce deals directly with other organisations (buyers) and is often used more than advertising. In the case of an industrial product, there may be relatively few potential buyers and a direct approach may be more successful. Industrial products are usually technical in nature and the client needs the expertise, advice and support of the sales team. Price will also be a key component – if a rival supplier can undercut the price, the buyer may be tempted to move. The role of price will depend on how differentiated the product is and on the product's perceived value.

Consumer markets

Consumer markets are more complex than industrial markets, and come in many more forms. One particular difference in marketing mixes is seen between mass markets and niche markets.

Mass markets

If a firm is competing in a mass market it may compete primarily on availability. In the snack chocolate market, for example, a product is unlikely to achieve a significant market share unless it is available in the many places people pick up such products – ranging from newsagents and petrol stations to high street stores and supermarkets. Price, taste and packaging will all be important, but if the product is not available for impulse purchasing, it will find it difficult to earn a place in the market.

Questions   PROGRESS CHECK

1 Differentiate between the marketing mixes typical of industrial and consumer markets (see table 6.2).
2 Assess the possible importance of branding in the industrial goods market.

Niche markets

Niche market products, on the other hand, are ones that the customer may be willing to search for and they may spend time over the purchasing decision. A firm which is able to create a strong enough brand image is likely to dominate a niche sufficiently to ensure high returns. For example, the Body Shop developed the niche market of environmentally friendly cosmetics and, in the process, became a leading brand in the field, even when other producers tried to imitate the products and copy the key selling points. The success of the firm over two decades rested largely on its ability to maintain its brand leadership. In terms of a marketing

FEATURE	INDUSTRIAL GOODS	CONSUMER GOODS
nature of the buyer	professional; often products are bought by people whose job is to purchase supplies for the firm	amateur
number of buyers	few	many
importance of packaging	likely to be low	likely to be higher

Table 6.2 A comparison of industrial and consumer markets

strategy, then, the central elements were product and store image, and product differentiation.

KEY TERM

Niche product
focuses on a small
segment of the market.

The marketing mix and the product life cycle

At different stages of a product's life, different marketing approaches are likely to be needed. As seen in Chapter 5, each stage of a product's life has its own characteristics. These stages are examined now in terms of the likely and appropriate features of the marketing mix.

Introduction

The launch of a product into a new marketplace tends to be associated with slow growth and minimal profits. The firm must decide how it is going to bring the product to the attention of consumers. It could advertise heavily or rely on word of mouth to get the product known. Selling at a low initial cost may encourage take up by customers, or a premium price may create an image that tempts first time buyers. The deciding factors between these alternatives might be: the product itself; its intended image or the level of competition in the market.

The basic aim for the introduction phase, however it is approached, is to allow the product to find a place in the market.

Growth

This stage is indicated by a rapid growth in sales and an increasing profit. Pricing policies can be adjusted. If the product was introduced at a low initial price, this might be raised to the market level. A high initial price can be reduced to encourage even higher sales. To prolong sales growth, the product can be developed and improved, and new markets can be found either geographically or by usage. Distribution can be widened at this stage.

The strategy for the growth stage is to develop the product's markets as fully as possible.

Maturity

Sales growth slows down and profits level out in the maturity phase. Firms will attempt to renew sales growth possibly by innovating the product, such as by reformulating or repackaging. Advertising and promotion can be used extensively to renew interest in the product. Towards the end of this stage when the first indications of a real decline are apparent, the firm can develop extension strategies, such as targeting new market segments or developing new uses for the product.

In maturity, the firm is aiming to regenerate interest in the product and to keep it thriving.

Decline

The final stage is characterised by falling sales and profits as the strategies attempted in the maturity phase finally lose out to developments from outside the firm. A firm can continue its attempts to extend the life of the product as it did in the maturity stage or it could reduce marketing spending on the product to increase the profit margin for the remainder of its life. Ultimately, the company is likely to replace the product with one more suited to the current state of the market.

The aim in the decline phase is to minimise the adverse impact on the firm, its profits and its workers of the failing product.

The suitability of strategies mentioned above is highly dependent on the exact situation being faced by an individual firm. Each circumstance is different and the marketplace ever changing. The marketing strategies adopted must be flexible enough to make the most of the opportunities available at a given moment.

PROGRESS CHECK

Questions

1 Analyse the ways in which the marketing mix may be adapted at different stages of the product life cycle.
2 How far is it possible to plan ahead by using the product life cycle as a basis for future marketing mixes?

Which element of the marketing mix is the most important?

It is easy to say that each of the elements of the marketing mix, whether your definition is the four Ps or whether you take the broader view and include other aspects, is of vital importance. After all, if any aspect of the mix is inappropriate, the whole marketing strategy is likely to collapse. For example, a new soft drink may have just the right taste for its intended market and be supported by advertising that creates an image which will appeal to consumers. However, poor distribution or too high a price may prevent people from buying the product, and hence it is likely to fail.

All elements of the marketing mix are crucial. It is not possible to be successful without a product or service, if consumers do not know what you are offering, or if they cannot get hold of it. You cannot make a profit without a price.

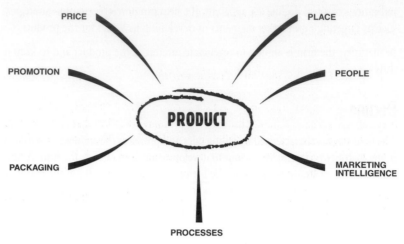

Figure 6.2 The product as the central aspect of the marketing mix

The product as the most important element of the mix

Although each aspect of the mix is undeniably important and all are interrelated, the product or service itself might be considered of primary importance. A poor product is highly unlikely to succeed. A good product may fail due to short-comings in the other elements of the mix, but may be strong enough to survive whilst these other factors are altered. An inappropriate price for a product can quickly be remedied and a poor distribution network can also be altered. If the product itself is fundamentally inappropriate (poorly designed, failing to meet customer needs or too expensive to produce, for example) it may be less easy to put things right.

By considering a typical manufacturing firm, it can be seen just how much time and effort goes into the design, development, testing and production of the finished articles. To stress the importance of the product within the marketing mix, the components are sometimes pictured as in figure 6.2, with the product as the central aspect and the other elements in a supporting role. This is not to diminish the importance of the other aspects of the marketing mix. To achieve a coherent marketing mix which allows the firm to fulfil its marketing objectives and its ultimate business goals, all the factors must work together in harmony. Nevertheless, it can be argued that they build around the product itself.

The relative importance of the different elements depends on the particular circumstances facing the firm. For example, in a recession consumers may be more price sensitive, may be less concerned about packaging and may switch away from heavily branded items to own label products.

The elements of the marketing mix are interdependent. Once a firm settles on one aspect, this narrows down the range of options available for the other elements. Deciding to portray a high class image, for example, restricts the pricing decision; the price should be high.

Small firms with limited production capacity would not aim for the same scale of distribution as a multinational.

What makes a product successful?

As well as the support of an appropriate marketing mix, the one key factor that is necessary for success in the marketplace is the ability to differentiate one product from all the others that are available. By demonstrating that their product is different from the others, producers are providing consumers with a reason to buy from them, instead of from competitors.

The differentiating factor, often called the **Unique Selling Point** or **Unique Selling Proposition (USP)**, can be real or imagined.

Real USP

A physical difference between one product and the others, perhaps protected by a patent, gives the consumer a real benefit. Unfortunately for many producers, however, there is little that modern technology is unable to imitate closely, even when direct copying is illegal. Real differences are likely to be short lived and constant development is likely to be needed before consumers accept that the firm is truly innovative and has a technological edge over its competitors.

Imagined or perceived USP

This is where the difference is created and held in the minds of consumers. Effective advertising can give a product an image that appeals to a certain market segment, either by using carefully chosen imagery, by association with other items or a well known personality. The downside to the creation of an imagined USP is the cost of creating the image, often with expensive television advertising over an extended period of time, and the risk of losing consumer confidence if the product, once bought, fails to live up to the image created.

For a marketing strategy to be successful, it must focus on the product and its USP. Most markets, certainly for consumer goods, have a large number of suppliers, all competing for market share. For a firm, the keys to marketing success in a competitive market are:

- to ensure that consumers are able to distinguish its product from all the others

- to ensure that the product is supported by a coherent and consistent marketing mix

- to ensure sufficient flexibility to be able to change the mix as and when external factors change

- to ensure quality in all aspects of the business.

However, success also depends on what the competitors are doing and the external environment. Although there are many factors which a firm can influence or control, such as its promotional strategy and its distribution, there are other factors

FACT FILE

The Volvo car brand has traditionally targeted consumers for whom the protection of self and family is a primary concern. This is reflected in a product with steel beams in the roof and protective side panels. It is also shown in a promotion which used crash survivors testifying that their Volvos saved their lives.

KEY POINTS

An effective marketing mix will be:

- coherent, in that all elements are pulling in the same direction
- manageable, in terms of the resources and capabilities of the firm
- focused, in its support of the product.

FACT FILE

Unable to get to the market via the usual department stores, Avon cosmetics identified a new distribution channel and sold its products door to door.

KEY TERMS

Shopping good
is one which consumers 'shop around' for before buying, such as washing machines and televisions. Consumers often compare prices before buying.

Convenience item
is a good which consumers tend to buy from the nearest outlet, such as milk or cigarettes.

which are beyond its control, such as interest rates and new product development by the competition. The winning firms are those which are continually monitoring their environment so that they can anticipate change and are able to respond rapidly. Theodore Levitt wrote about 'marketing myopia' which describes organisations that are so short-sighted they fail to identify the changes going on in their markets. Successful companies keep well informed and have effective marketers ready to adapt the marketing strategies and mix accordingly.

PROGRESS CHECK

What determines the success of a firm's marketing mix?

Price as the most important element of the mix

We have stressed throughout this chapter that all the elements of the mix must be integrated with each other for the product or service to succeed. What consumers are really looking for is **good value for money**: this means that the price charged must match the benefits offered. If the benefits are high enough people will be willing to pay a lot. The problems only come when the price is high but the benefits are not – this leads to customer dissatisfaction. So the *price relative to the benefits* available is more important that the price itself.

Having said this, there are times when consumers become more sensitive to price. For example, price is likely to be more important in a recession when consumers may have less income. Price is also more important for shopping goods (consumers tend to make direct comparisons of similar products) than for convenience items. Consumers are more likely to compare prices if the goods are close substitutes and are not heavily branded; if, by comparison, the goods are highly differentiated and consumers cannot easily switch from one to the other, the price is less likely to be a major factor.

PROGRESS CHECK

How important is price in determining the success of a product?

Distribution and the marketing mix

Distribution is often neglected as an element of the marketing mix and, yet, is crucial to a product's success. Effective distribution has a direct impact on a firm's costs, its ability to respond to the market, its coverage of the market and the overall positioning of the product. Just think about a product such as a soft drink. Many of us go to the nearest shop and buy one of several brands that we are happy to drink. If one brand is not there, we buy another one instead. It is absolutely essential in this type of market for the producer to get their product widely distributed, so wherever the consumer is, the product is available. Coca Cola's mission is to have its products be 'within an arm's length of desire' – to decide on how effective they are, think how far you are from a bottle or can of coke at any moment in time. If you wanted to buy one now, where would you go? Companies such as Coca Cola and Pepsi fight fiercely over distribution channels such as fast food restaurants, sports clubs, retailers and within large organisations. Each company is eager to gain exclusive rights to the market.

Without an effective distribution channel, a firm will be unable to compete however good its product is. Many Western companies have complained that access to the Japanese market is extremely difficult and that this has prevented them competing. In the 1990s, for example, Kodak found it hard to get its products to the market in Japan and accused the Japanese government of protectionism; one of its arguments was that the Japanese government prevents the growth of many retailers and, because of limited space, they stock domestic products not foreign ones!

The power of distribution as a competitive weapon can be seen in the success of companies such as Direct Line (telephone insurance), First Direct (telephone banking) and Amazon.com (Internet bookseller). These firms have developed innovative ways of getting their products to the market. This has differentiated their offering and enabled them to make savings, allowing them to offer better value for money. The growth of the Internet may mean that traditional distribution channels (e.g. high street banking, local travel agents) are seriously under attack.

KEY POINTS

Consumers are more likely to be price conscious when:

- the goods are similar and easy to compare
- the goods are not heavily differentiated
- it is easy to switch from one good to another
- consumers' incomes are low.

FACT FILE

In the 1990s, Unilever struggled to establish its position in China. In the washing powder and shampoo markets, for example, the local manufacturers tend to dominate, followed by Procter and Gamble. Unilever has tended to follow behind because of relatively weak distribution, meaning it cannot get its products into the shops for consumers to buy. In order to combat this, it announced a major restructuring of its distribution network.

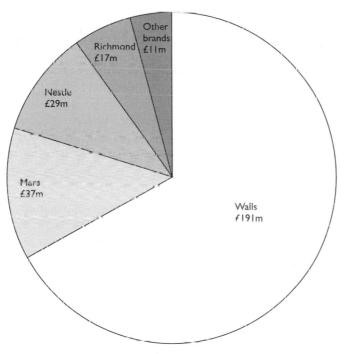

Figure 6.3 Share of wrapped impulse ice cream market, 1998
Source: Mintel; Financial Times 20 July 1999

KEY POINTS

Distribution is more likely to be important:

- in a very cost competitive market
- for convenience items
- if it can differentiate a firm's offering.

PROGRESS CHECK

Discuss ways in which the distribution of a product or service can affect its competitiveness.

FACT FILE

In 1999, the Competition Commission said it believed that Walls had a scale monopoly with more than 25% of the impulse ice cream market and that it had adopted anti-competitive practices (see Figure 6.3). These included a distribution system (Walls Direct) which made it difficult for competitors to enter the market — other ice cream makers found it difficult to get their products in the shops because Walls had given owners fridges and had them stocked with Walls products.

Is promotion important?

The promotion of a product or service communicates something about it to consumers. Without promotion, potential customers would not even know about the product. The greatest product in the world will not sell if no-one knows it exists. However, what matters is not necessarily the *amount* of promotion a firm undertakes but the *quality* of the promotion. This involves constructing an appropriate promotional mix. Many people focus exclusively on advertising when asked about promotion but, in fact, promotional activities are more far reaching than this; for example, they include personal selling, public relations and sales promotions. In the case of an industrial good, for example, personal selling could be much more relevant and effective than advertising. Sales promotions may work well for certain consumer goods, but may be less appropriate for some services (e.g. education services and legal advice). A firm must, therefore, consider its promotional aims (to inform? to persuade? to increase long-term awareness? to increase impulse buys?), select from the range of promotional tools and then devise an appropriate mix. Promotion must fit with the other marketing mix elements – a discount on an exclusive product may actually damage the brand, rather than enhance it, for example.

PROGRESS CHECK

Discuss the factors which might determine the right promotional mix for a product.

Is the marketing mix under a firm's control?

The actual mix of tools used by a firm in its marketing is, of course, decided by its managers. In this sense, the mix is under the firm's control. Managers set the price, decide on the precise nature of the product, decide how and where to promote it and how they want to distribute it. At the same time, some factors are out of their control: they may not be able to distribute where they want to if competitors have signed exclusive contracts to use these channels. Also, changes in the mix may be forced on the firm – in a declining market, a firm may have to reduce its product range; legislation may prevent certain types of advertising. In this situation, managers still have control of the mix but have to react to external change.

Summary chart

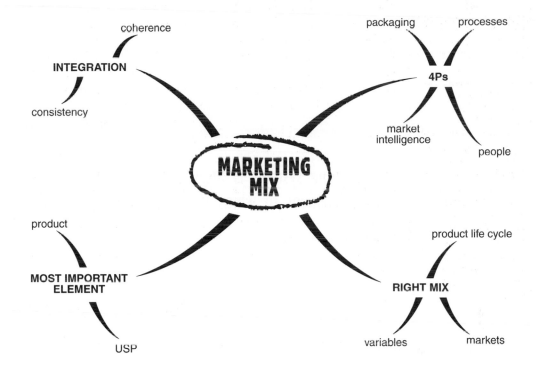

Figure 6.4 Key elements of the marketing mix

Approaching exam questions: The marketing mix

A firm selling industrial heating systems is attempting to break into the consumer market. Assess the extent to which it may need to change its marketing mix.

(40 marks)

Despite the discussion in this chapter, it is perfectly acceptable in an essay to limit a discussion of the marketing mix to the traditional four Ps. Some credit may be gained by indicating that you are aware of additional features of the mix, but the point does not have to be stressed – it would add little to the answer of a specific question such as this. However, be wary of simply listing the four Ps and describing each one in detail. This is a very common mistake – make sure you explain how the mix has to be *adapted* to a particular market and consumers.

'To what extent . . .' questions always require a two-sided answer indicating, in this case, what factors may have to change and the reasons why some factors may stay the same. Normally, the conclusion will be that change must occur 'to some extent'.

The reasons why things may have to change could include the facts that:

■ any new market will have different requirements and, hence, a different mix will be appropriate

■ consumer markets usually have a greater degree of competition, so the firm must be more reactive to the changing needs of its customers

■ relationships with consumers will not be close, as they often are in industrial markets, giving promotion a greater emphasis

■ distribution networks may need developing.

On the other hand, some basic essentials remain the same, such as:

■ the product must still reflect the needs of the customer

■ the customer remains the basis for decision-making

■ the whole mix must be coherent and integrated.

In conclusion, there are likely to be changes in the marketing mix, although the fundamental points are likely to remain the same. The change will be one of emphasis, rather than a complete remodelling of the marketing system.

Evaluate the possible contribution of a USP to a product's success.

(11 marks)

Evaluation questions ask the candidate to weigh up evidence to arrive at a justified conclusion. In this case, he or she has to give evidence of how a USP contributes to a product's success, together with counter arguments, perhaps to show that a USP *alone* cannot guarantee success.

A conclusion is likely to show that a USP is important to a product's success, but that other issues have a role to play as well.

The ways in which a USP contributes to a product's success could include:

■ it is a differentiating feature to make the product stand out in the marketplace

■ it may help create a superior image in the minds of consumers which may be long lasting

■ it may be a tangible benefit for the consumer, encouraging them to return to the product again.

On the other hand a USP may not be sufficient by itself to ensure success because:

■ although a USP is part of the product, all other aspects of the marketing mix must be present and correct

■ some products reach a satisfactory level of success without any obvious differentiating factor.

In conclusion then, a USP is unlikely to be the sole reason for a product's success. It is possible to question what is meant by success – does it imply the product becomes the market leader, or can a satisfactory level of sales also be counted as a success?

Is it possible to justify the inclusion of market intelligence as part of the marketing mix?

(11 marks)

In order to justify something, the writer must present evidence both for and against the proposition. In this case, that means giving reasons why marketing intelligence should be included as part of the marketing mix, and reasons why it shouldn't. This is followed by an evaluation of the arguments, together with a judgement one way or the other.

Possible reasons for including marketing intelligence in the marketing mix are:

■ it should be the basis for all marketing decisions

■ as market conditions change, market intelligence can inform the rest of the marketing mix.

On the other hand:

■ the four Ps model provides a simple framework – adding other ingredients may only add to the complexity

■ the four Ps are marketing decisions regarding the sale of a product, marketing intelligence goes much further than this

■ the four Ps model has never excluded marketing intelligence. It was never intended to be a 'stand-alone' decision-making model, so marketing intelligence, in effect, was always present.

In conclusion, it is possible that the argument is an academic one. The four Ps model was always meant to take account of all other relevant information and factors, so marketing intelligence was always a central part of the marketing decision-making process. Nevertheless, by including marketing intelligence in the marketing mix, marketing decision-makers remind themselves that the four Ps is a very simplistic model that must be treated with caution. It is possible to conclude this question with a decision either way.

To what extent can firms change a product's marketing mix?

(11 marks)

As with all 'to what extent' questions, the answer must include arguments looking at both sides of the case before a final decision is reached.

In this case, the question is asking for a consideration of how much of the marketing mix is determined by outside factors, and how much is within the control of the business. Although there are factors on both sides, an issue like this will differ greatly from one firm to another. There is, therefore, much scope for a strong conclusion emphasising the factors that can change in different firms.

Possible reasons why the marketing mix *can* be controlled by the firm are:

■ decisions on all aspects of the marketing mix are set internally – the firm can choose any combination it likes

■ as circumstances change, successful firms change their own marketing mix to prosper, rather than having changes forced on them by outside agencies.

On the other hand:

■ if a firm wishes to be successful, it must respond to the market, so its decisions are heavily constrained by outside forces

■ some aspects of the mix rely on external agreements, such as distribution networks, retail prices and product specification, so the firm can not always decide these things by itself.

In conclusion, the degree to which a firm can determine its own marketing mix depends to a large degree on the individual circumstances. A market leader may have greater flexibility than a market follower; a strong brand name may allow more freedom than a me-too product; and an innovative firm may be able to change its products more often, and with more success, than firms noted for their stability.

Student answers

To what extent is the success of the marketing mix dependent on the quality of market intelligence available to the firm?

(11 marks)

Student answer

The success of the marketing mix is highly dependent on marketing intelligence. If the firm does not have all the information it needs, it will not be able to make the right decisions. For example, if a firm did not know that a rival had cut the price of a product by 10p, it may decide to keep its price high. It may lose customers to the cheaper product and so lose profit. Also, it will not know about new products coming into the market and may lose sales if it does not make a new product of its own.

Marker's comments

Although this candidate clearly recognises the importance of marketing intelligence, he or she does not use this to great effect. The points made are very shallow, and there is little evidence given to support the views expressed. There is no consideration of any reasons why the firm may not be dependent on marketing intelligence as required by a 'to what extent' question.

Marks Content 1/2, Application & Analysis 3/6, Evaluation 0/3. Total = 4

Analyse the possible importance of the workforce to a firm's marketing success.

(9 marks)

Student answer

The workforce has been called a firm's greatest asset. If a firm has a high class workforce, this is likely to be apparent to consumers.

For example, a high quality workforce will produce high quality products which meet the required specifications and suffer from few, if any, defects. Customers will see the firm as one that produces quality and reliable goods and will return to the firm in the future for more goods. The workforce is helping promote the name and image of the firm.

On the other hand, a workforce alone will not make a product successful in the market. The best product in the world will not sell well if the price is wrong or the distribution network fails to deliver the product to the right place at the right time. All the elements of the marketing mix have to be right if the firm's products are to be successful.

End of section questions

1 Analyse the role of each of the four Ps in the marketing of a product or service of your choice.

(9 marks)

2 To what extent does the marketing mix determine the success of a product?

(11 marks)

3 Discuss the possible importance of a USP to the success of a product.

(11 marks)

4 Examine how the marketing of industrial goods may differ from the marketing of consumer goods.

(9 marks)

5 Analyse the factors which might influence a firm's marketing mix.

(9 marks)

6 To what extent is price the most important element of the marketing mix?

(11 marks)

7 Analyse the way in which the marketing mix may be adapted at different stages of the product life cycle.

(9 marks)

8 Discuss the possible impact on the marketing mix of new competitors entering the market.

(11 marks)

9 Discuss the ways in which a firm might adapt the buying process of its product to gain a competitive advantage.

(11 marks)

10 Discuss how the people within an organisation can contribute to its marketing.

(11 marks)

Essays

1 To what extent is the product itself the most important element of the marketing mix?

(40 marks)

2 To what extent is the marketing mix governed by the stage the product has reached in its life cycle?

(40 marks)

3 'All elements of the marketing mix have an equal importance.' Assess this statement.

(40 marks)

4 To what extent is a firm free to choose its own marketing mix?

(40 marks)

5 Evaluate the contribution of the marketing mix to the achievement of a firm's strategic aims.

(40 marks)

CHAPTER 7

Recent issues

Introduction

As has been stressed throughout this book, marketing takes place in an ever changing environment. Society is constantly changing and the pace of that change gets faster and faster. With the marketing emphasis on consumer orientation, these changes must be reflected in a firm's marketing strategy if it is to hold or improve its competitive position.

In the past, some firms have faced changes in demands from consumers with changing tastes, incomes and lifestyles, while other markets have remained relatively static. As the twentieth century drew to a close, the pace of change intensified, and the scale of the changes increased. The key factors that have caused the marketing world to undergo such massive movements include:

- the need for global marketing

- increasing ethical awareness and concerns of consumers

- the rate of change of technology.

The combination of these factors has caused, and will continue to cause, fundamental shifts in the marketing environment for businesses. The following discussion highlights the extent of the changes that firms' marketing functions have had to go through in recent times in order to maintain a competitive position in its market.

Faced with a rapidly changing future, firms need to consider whether:

- they have prepared for change

- they have the right resources

- they have key personnel in place

- they have a clear aim.

> **In a changing world firms may need to become more nimble to survive.**

Global marketing

For businesses, the world is becoming a smaller place. Travel and transportation is becoming quicker and easier, communications can be instantaneous to any part of the world and trade barriers are breaking down. The consequence is that businesses in one country have tremendous opportunities to broaden their markets into foreign countries. The challenge facing marketers is to be able to cross the physical and cultural barriers which divide international markets, so that their products can successfully compete with foreign products.

How can firms prepare effectively for changes in the scope of their market?

Some of the key questions that may arise are:

■ *'Should a marketing mix be the same across the world or adapted to different markets?'* There are many theorists who argue that, with the 'shrinking' of the world, global standardisation is inevitable. Over time and as economies develop, the buying patterns of consumers will blend into one another and national differences may disappear. Kellogg, the American breakfast cereal producer, has been very influential in changing consumption patterns in countries outside the United States. In France, for example, breakfast cereals were almost unheard of, and market research suggested that the market was closed to companies like Kellogg. Today, there is a growing demand for breakfast cereals across France.

On the other hand, some companies, such as Coca Cola, do change their products from one country to the next. The recipe for Coke is changed to suit local tastes – the brand in the US is much sweeter than in the UK, whilst in India the product's herbs and flavourings are given more emphasis. Car manufacturers tend to take a half-way approach – it would be too expensive to develop and build completely different vehicles for different markets, but a single, global model is likely to appeal to no-one. Nissan, for example, sells in 75 different markets, but has eight different chassis designs. The Ford Mondeo was designed with key features from different markets in mind in an effort to make its appeal as broad as possible.

In short, there is no evidence to suggest that one technique is better than any other. As with many business concepts, the marketing mix adopted will depend on many factors, such as the type of product, the degree of competition, the reputation of the firm and/or the brand, and the state of the economy into which the product is to be launched.

Can it be right to sell different products under the same name in different markets, as done by firms such as Coca Cola?

■ *'Should products be launched simultaneously in all countries, or should a launch be staggered over time?'* In practice, most companies producing consumer goods tend to launch a new product in one or two markets at a time rather than attempt to launch a product across a range of countries at a single time. Many high-tech products, such as DVD players, reached the market in Japan before reaching the UK. Hollywood films are often seen in the United States weeks or months before they arrive in this country. For example, *Star Wars Episode One* was launched in the US in May 1999, in the UK in July 1999 and in Spain in August 1999.

The advantage for firms is that it is easier to launch in one market at a time. Effort and concentration can be focused to ensure the best possible entry into the market. For technical products especially, any teething problems become apparent in a single market and can be corrected prior to launch elsewhere.

However, a single product launch, moving sequentially from one country to the next, takes up a lot of time that may be better used developing the next new product. Competitors may see the product and have time to develop a response before it actually arrives in their market, so that some of the advantages of developing an innovative product may be lost.

It is likely that a firm will attempt to launch a product simultaneously in several markets where there is a lot of competition or when the product is relatively cheap. Intel, in the highly competitive market of computer chips, tends to launch its new products internationally at the same time to keep the product ahead of competitors.

KEY TERMS

'Sprinkler launch'
a product that is launched simultaneously in all markets.

'Waterfall launch'
a product launched sequentially in one market after another.

■ '*How far can cultural differences be taken into account?*' When a firm enters a global market, it has to cope with many differences. Some are quite obvious: prices have to be converted to a different currency and any literature has to be translated into a different language. There are also less tangible differences, due to the cultural differences between people of different countries. It is possible for cultures to be so different that common practices in one country can cause offence and have grave consequences for business success in another. Charles Handy, in his book *The Empty Raincoat*, tells of the time he had just completed some difficult negotiations for an oil company with the firm's Chinese dealers. After shaking hands on the deal, Handy began to fill out the paperwork in preparation for signing the deal, much to the concern of the Chinese delegates. The explanation for the problem was as follows:

'If we agreed them, [the figures] why do you want a legal document? It makes me suspect that you have got more out of this agreement than I have, and you are going to use the weight of the law to enforce your terms. In my culture ... a good agreement is self-enforcing because both parties go away smiling and are happy to see that each of us is smiling. If one smiles and the other scowls, the agreement will not stick, lawyers or no lawyers.' (*The Empty Raincoat*, Charles Handy, Hutchinson, 1994)

Without knowing it, the Western negotiator had caused offences to the other party in the negotiations and almost cost his company the deal that had been worked for over many months. If a company is attempting to broaden its operations into other countries, especially over a great distance, it must take the time to find out about local customs and methods of business operation. Equally important, is to ensure that such information is available to all necessary workers in the organisation.

British Airways is one company that has attempted to develop an awareness among its employees of the cultural differences that can exist between passengers from different countries. Its 'Kaleidoscope' programme aims to raise awareness of cultural differences amongst all its 14,000 cabin crew in an attempt to avoid causing offence to passengers from abroad, however innocently. It was a similar attempt to cater for cultural differences that led BA to change the design of the tail fins of some of its aircraft from the traditional Union Jack design to ethnic designs from countries across the world. After a couple of years, BA bowed to public pressure in the UK and returned half of its fleet to the traditional design. The lesson for marketers is clear: the attempt to appeal to international markets can help to boost performance in those countries, but the firm should not neglect its roots. For a firm like BA, the attempt to appeal to the 60% of its customers who live outside the UK had to be balanced against the fact that the UK is still its biggest single market.

There are no simple answers for dealing with foreign customers and markets, but the answer will always lie in having sufficient information to allow appropriate decisions to be made.

PROGRESS CHECK

To what extent should a firm treat the world as one single market?

Marketing ethics

Ethics in business has been one of the major areas of change and development throughout the 1990s. Concerns for the environment and the rights of stakeholders have been at the forefront of the debate in this area.

As far as the marketing function is concerned, the key ethical debates centre around these questions:

- Is it right for marketing to play on people's fears and unrealistic aspirations?

- How far ought marketing be allowed to create demand amongst consumers rather than merely satisfying them?

- Should marketing be allowed to cater for any products that consumers demand?

Playing on fears

Consumers can be greatly influenced by public figures (and their images), such as actors and sports stars. To many people, the regular exposure of such individuals and their life styles on television and in magazines creates a desire for self improvement, to be more like the day's popular heroes. Marketing, it is alleged, plays on such aspirations in order to encourage the purchase of products, some of which may be inappropriate for the consumer. The popular media portrayal of women tends to suggest that all women ought to be happy, successful and thin, with perfect make-up, designer clothes and so on. The belief is that such portrayals can lead consumers to buy products which are out of their price range, possibly leading to debt. There may even be associated health risks, such as anorexia.

Although such an opinion appears logical, there is little hard evidence to support it as yet. The counter argument suggests that people are not as gullible as some would make out and that most people are able to separate the make-believe world of television and films from the real world. Nevertheless, the constant barrage of similar messages from a range of sources is a very powerful force, and there is little doubt that public attitudes have changed rapidly at the same time as television has become a more pervasive part of everyday life. Where, for example, has the growth in sales of men's cosmetics and toiletries really come from?

Creating demand

A commonly stated aim of marketing is to meet the needs of consumers. However, questions can be raised as to whether these needs actually arise in the consumer, or if they are being created by clever marketing. Did consumers actually want mobile phones with changeable, coloured casings, or was this a gimmick to create a unique selling point for a product? There are many examples of products that seem to create their own demand, fulfilling the business need to capture market share, without ever being requested or required by the consumer.

Does this represent a manipulation of consumers by firms? It may be argued that, rather than creating a demand, firms are *anticipating* changes in demand. The fact that such products catch on may be taken as proof that they fulfil a requirement of the marketplace. Against this is the fact that many new and innovative products do not succeed, suggesting that the prediction of future demand is, at best, an imprecise science. The suspicion remains that many new developments are aimed, as much at creating a demand amongst consumers, as fulfilling existing needs.

Limits to products

If marketing exists to fulfil the needs and demands of consumers, to what extent should firms be absolved of the responsibility for those products? Millions of people in the UK demand cigarettes, and yet there is a clear link between the product and long-term health risks. In the United States, tobacco companies are being sued because of the ill health caused by their products (it is alleged that they knew about the health risks a long time before they made these public). The question then becomes one of where the boundary lies between catering for demand and being responsible for the outcome of that demand.

It may seem obvious where this line should be drawn in clear cut cases, such as the sale of weapons or the targeting of 'alcopop' alcoholic drinks at young people. The boundary is less clear when it comes to other products with a less obvious negative influence. Is it right for a firm to sell the dream of becoming a multimillionaire, as the National Lottery does? The chances of winning are around 14 million to one against, and the people who spend the largest proportion of their income in pursuit of the dream are those on the lowest incomes.

It is possible to claim that marketers are only interested in these questions because they help to achieve overall targets, such as sales growth and market penetration. Being seen to be concerned about ethics can produce positive publicity for a firm or the brand names of its products.

On one level, it can be argued that the ethical stances being taken by many firms is just a cynical ploy to promote a favourable public image. On the other hand, does this really matter? Whatever motivates a firm, the fact that they are doing all they can to be seen to be acting ethically may be sufficient to promote such behaviour and embed it in the culture of businesses. Once this happens, the ethics of business and marketing will have changed forever, hopefully to the benefit of every member of society.

PROGRESS CHECK

Is ethical marketing a waste of time or does it make good business sense?

Technological developments

New technology is quickly becoming part of our everyday lives. E-mail and the Internet are in regular use and their penetration into ordinary people's lives is increasing steadily. The business and marketing potential of these products is becoming more and more apparent as some astonishing success stories are widely reported in the press. Amazon.com, the Internet bookseller, reportedly sells over $150 m of books every year.

However, for every major success story there will be many others who have tried and failed. The challenge facing marketing managers is to adapt profitably to the range of possibilities offered by the new technologies. Some of these possibilities are discussed below.

Finding out what customers want

The developments in technology make it possible for firms to listen to and understand their consumers more easily and at a reduced cost. For example, EPOS which links cash registers to a customer database can provide a quick and easy way to track the buying habits of customers. Decisions based on this type of information can be made efficiently and, hopefully, with a greater accuracy than in the past, suggesting that marketing can be much more focused than ever before.

Market segmentation

The sheer size of the global community embodied by the Internet means that all manner of people with different interests, hobbies and lifestyles are accessible. Advertising on the net can be targeted to appeal to those groups most likely to be interested in the product. Again, the implication for marketing is that potential consumers can be reached in a more cost effective and efficient manner than ever before.

Direct marketing

If there is one area of 'traditional' marketing that makes use of a range of skills which may be useful for e-commerce, it is direct marketing. The Internet allows firms to have direct access to individual consumers in a way unprecedented by existing standards. By combining the skills of direct marketing with the capabilities of the Internet, a firm could present its potential customers with information about products which is tailored specifically to suit their needs.

Of course, the impact of new technologies on marketing must be seen in a wider context. The potential advantages to a single company also apply to its competitors, whether they already compete in the same marketplace or, with the increase in globalisation, whether they are becoming direct competitors for the first time.

It is also possible to overstate the current importance of the technology. In 1998, it is estimated that only 10% of homes in the UK are linked to the Internet. Although this number is predicted to grow in the future, it may be some time before the majority of people are regular users of the Internet and even longer before consumers are regular users of e-commerce services.

At this stage, these new technologies are growth areas. All firms need to be making preparations if they are to be in a position to compete successfully in the future.

PROGRESS CHECK

Should marketing departments welcome or fear new technology?

Summary chart

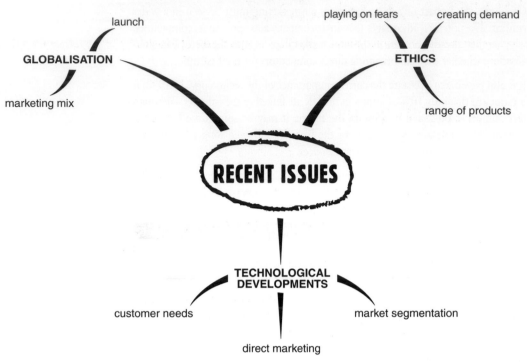

Figure 7.1 Key issues for the future

CHAPTER 8

Numerical data

1. Hairlucinations

Total for this question: 40 marks

DEB plc is a manufacturer of a wide range of fast moving consumer goods. The firm is concerned about one of its products, Hairlucinations – a range of hair colouring gels. Although Hairlucinations has enjoyed a degree of market dominance in the past due to its quality image, the product has recently been losing market share to similar, lower priced products from its competitors. The firm has to decide whether or not to reduce the price of Hairlucinations in an attempt to re-establish the product's dominance in the marketplace.

In your role as a management consultant, write a report to the marketing manager of DEB plc, based on the information below, recommending whether or not it should reduce the price of the Hairlucinations range.

(2 marks are included for report format)

Appendices

- **Appendix A:**   market research results
- **Appendix B:**   statement of confidence levels
- **Appendix C:**   backdata
- **Appendix D:**   average price elasticity of demand
- **Appendix E:**   price:sales correlation data

Appendix A: market research results from a random sample of 500 female shoppers

| | HAIR COLOURANT USED MOST FREQUENTLY | | | |
	HAIRLUCINATION	COMPETITORS	NONE	TOTAL
No. of respondents	86	223	191	500
Definitely willing to try Hairlucinations at a lower price	100%	47.1%	2.1%	39%
Definitely willing to buy Hairlucinations regularly at a lower price	100%	13.9%	1.6%	24.4%
Believes all hair products are very much the same	53.5%	78.5%	94.2%	80.2%

Appendix B: statement of confidence levels

The company's statisticians have calculated a 68% confidence level for the research results in Appendix A.

Appendix C: backdata

Reliability of past research results when compared with observed buyer behaviour

| | FROM RESEARCH | | ACTUAL CHANGE |
	WILL TRY	WILL CHANGE	
Deknotting shampoo	+ 6%	+ 1%	− 5%
Home Streaks kit	+24%	+24%	+24%
Insta-perm	+47%	+39%	+68%
Bucks Frizz	+10%	+ 9%	+ 5%
Hairlucinations	+26%	+ 8%	?

Appendix D: average price elasticity of demand

Hair products (general) − 3.4

Hair products (DEB plc) − 1.9

All products (DEB plc) − 2.5

Hairlucinations – price has not been changed in 3 years

Appendix E: price:sales correlation data for DEB plc hair products

(data collected at various dates in recent years)

PRICE COMPARED WITH MARKET AVERAGE	SALES LEVEL COMPARED WITH MARKET AVERAGE
+6%	−2%
+6%	−4%
+5%	=
+3%	−1%
+3%	−10%
+1%	+3%
=	+2%
=	−3%
−1%	−5%
−3%	−5%
−5%	−12%
−5%	−10%

2. CNC Ltd

Total for this question: 40 marks

CNC Ltd is a producer of alcoholic drinks, particularly spirits. The firm holds high hopes for one of its newer products, O'Knorrs' Irish Cream.

As a Management Consultant, you have been asked to provide an outline marketing strategy for the medium term to enable O'Knorrs' to become a leading brand among 18–28 year olds in the CD social category. The following data has been supplied to assist you.

(2 marks are available for report format)

Appendices

- **Appendix A:** brand history for O'Knorrs' Irish Cream
- **Appendix B:** market trends
- **Appendix C:** distribution channels
- **Appendix D:** conversion rates
- **Appendix E:** IDQV analysis for O'Knorrs' brand

Appendix A: brand history for O'Knorrs' Irish Cream

	SALES REVENUE (£M)	MARKET SHARE (%)	ADVERTISING EXPENDITURE (£M)	PROFITS (£)
5 years ago	4.25	1.25	1.25	(3)
4 years ago	11.6	4.15	1	(1)
3 years ago	13.8	4.8	1	0.5
2 years ago	15.5	5.25	0.75	1.5
Last year	14.75	4.75	0.5	2

Appendix B: market trends

	3 YEARS AGO	LAST YEAR	THIS YEAR	NEXT YEAR (FORECAST)	3 YEARS' TIME (FORECAST)
Total market (m litres)	19	20	20.5	20.75	21.25
% of all spirits	8.75	8.55	8.7	8.75	8.85
O'Knorrs' market share (%)	4.15	5.25	4.75	5.15	5.75
O'Knorrs' revenue (£m)	11.6	15.5	14.75	16.75	19.85
O'Knorrs' advertising expenditure (£)	1	0.75	0.5	1.05	1.25

Appendix C: distribution channels

TYPE OF RETAILER	% OF TOTAL SALES	TREND
Grocery chains	12	Growing
Off licences	10	Potential growth
Independent retailers	15	Falling
Pubs/clubs	51	Fewer customers
Hotels, restaurants	12	Static
TOTAL	100	

Appendix D: conversion rates relating to product trials

	O'KNORRS' (%)		MAJOR COMPETITORS (%)	
	% OF TARGET GROUP (18–28 CDs)	CONVERSION RATE	% OF TARGET GROUP (18–28 CDs)	CONVERSION RATE
Awareness of product	25	–	80	–
Conversion of awareness to trying product	9	36	30	38
Conversion of trying product to regular usage	3	33	15	50

Appendix E: IDQV analysis for O'Knorrs' brand amongst the target group of 18–28 CDs

MEASURE	MAXIMUM SCORE	O'KNORRS'	MAJOR COMPETITORS
Impact	35	20	34
Differentiation	30	17	17
Quality	15	9	11
Value	20	15	13
Brand strength	100	61	75

3. North End Ducks

Total for this question: 30 marks

Read the following information and then answer the questions that follow.

North End Ducks is the name adopted by a group of small farms specialising in the rearing and sale of ducklings to up-market restaurants in the North West of England. The group is concerned about a recent decline in sales, as shown in table 8.1, and is planning to increase the level of its direct marketing within its market segment. There is a worry, however, that this may not be the most appropriate course of action. In the past, the main advertising push has taken place at the start of the year, so the marketing team is confident that the advertising spend for a year relates directly to that year's sales.

YEAR	SALES (£000)	ADVERTISING SPEND (£000)
1	112	7
2	140	10
3	155	8
4	168	4
5	147	4
6	132	6
7	134	8
8 (last year)	133	6

Table 8.1 Advertising spend and sales figures

1 (a) From the figures given above, construct a correlation graph to show the apparent relationship between sales and advertising expenditure.

(4 marks)

(b) On the basis of your graph from part a, what sort of relationship appears to exist between sales and advertising?

(2 marks)

2 (a) Calculate the apparent advertising elasticity of demand for years 7 to 8.

(3 marks)

(b) Consider whether there is likely to be a causal relationship between sales and advertising in this case. Justify your answer.

(7 marks)

3 Given the relationship you have described in question 2, present a reasoned strategy for increasing the sales of the North End Ducks group.

(8 marks)

4 Explain two factors the firm might consider when setting its advertising budget.

(6 marks)

4. The Revers-o-barrow

Total for this question: 30 marks

Newman Partnership is a firm specialising in the production of garden equipment. They have recently been considering the introduction of a new product, the 'Revers-o-barrow', which it considers to be a revolutionary type of wheelbarrow with the wheel at the back rather than the front, allowing the user to push down to move the barrow, rather than having to lift it.

Although the Partnership is aware that its products sell all year, it recognises that there is a considerable difference in sales at different times of the year. The following figures relate to the firm's total sales over the last three years.

(£000)	3 YEARS AGO	2 YEARS AGO	LAST YEAR
January–March	235	242	220
April–June	789	806	780
July–September	1,012	1,137	1,104
October–December	135	130	127

Table 8.2 Sales figures for Newman Partnership (£000s)

1   Calculate the annual sales for the Newman Partnership for the period shown.

(2 marks)

2   Calculate the percentage change in annual sales.

(2 marks)

3   What are the *average* per quarter sales in each of the 3 years?

(2 marks)

4   On the basis of the evidence, in which quarter would you recommend the firm launches the 'Revers-o-barrow'? Justify your answer.

(7 marks)

5   Outline two other pieces of information that could be useful before making decisions about a product launch for Revers-o-barrow.

(8 marks)

6   Discuss the view that it is essential that Newman Partnership launches a new product to survive.

(9 marks)

Examining tips

Introduction

Examination questions on marketing tend to be highly analytical and often ask you to devise strategies for the future, rather than comment on existing situations. Some questions require an initial definition, but in general there is little benefit to be had from the repetition of learned notes. More than any other area of a business studies course, marketing provides a set of tools for problem-solving and decision-making, rather than a body of knowledge to be thrown at any given question.

In terms of a *strategy* for approaching exam questions, the following points are all useful ideas which should help you produce higher quality answers.

Marketing strategy

As discussed in Chapter 2, the basis of marketing decision-making is determined by the overall marketing strategy. This, in turn, is derived from the firm's own aims and objectives. Any marketing decision has to be based on the firm's marketing strategy. Where the examiner has provided information on the marketing strategy, your writing should be tailored to achieving those goals. Even if the marketing strategy is not specifically outlined, there is usually sufficient information to allow you to draw up a strategy suitable for the firm in the question. (If there is no obvious strategy, this is worth commenting on!)

If you are required to develop a marketing strategy for a firm, you will only get limited marks for making *general* points on marketing. The strategy you select must be:

■ *relevant to the circumstances described in the question* – a firm with cash flow problems is not likely to respond with short-term spending measures, such as an advertising campaign

■ *consistent and coherent* – a firm with a high quality image is not likely to adopt a strategy of penetration pricing

■ *directed to achieve the aims of the company* – a firm aiming to expand its market share will not adopt a restricted distribution policy.

The specifics of the firm

Each firm is unique in its position, background and standing. A high quality answer to a marketing question will be tailored to the *specific* circumstances of the firm in the question. This is true whether the answer is for a detailed case study or for an essay with a single sentence question.

Before planning your answer, it is always useful to ask yourself the following questions about the internal and external circumstances of the firm.

Internal issues

■ What size is the firm?

■ What resources are available to the firm?

■ How important is this product to the whole firm?

External issues

■ Does the firm operate in mass or niche markets?

■ Is it a market leader or follower?

■ What are competitors likely to do?

In addition consider the timescale indicated by the question and ask:

■ What are the long and short-term issues?

By taking account of all the issues relating to a firm and its circumstances, your answer will not only be relevant and specific, it will also demonstrate high levels of analysis: you will have read the question carefully, understood the context and applied your knowledge.

Scientific decision-making

All good marketing decisions, in theory, follow the sort of marketing model described in Chapter 1. This circular framework (see page 14) presents a clear pattern: gathering information, applying that information to a particular problem, putting the plan into action and then reviewing the decision in the light of any new information as it becomes available.

In reality, there may be reasons why a firm will by-pass parts of the model. These might include the following:

■ In times of crisis, there may not be time to complete the whole process. Decisions have to be made on the basis of readily available data and past experience.

■ Unexpected events, although not crises, may not allow firms the luxury of the time needed to follow the textbook marketing model.

■ Decision-makers in a firm often have great experience of their marketplace, and may at times have a strong feeling or hunch that is not supported by tangible evidence. In such cases, the marketing model may be by-passed and decisions are made on a different basis. It must, however, be recognised that such actions present their own dangers, and are likely to increase the level of risk for the firm.

Strategy versus planning versus action

It is important that you are clear about the difference between each of these three levels of marketing. Questions can ask about any of the three, and your answer must relate to that aspect. Although the issues are complex, simple definitions are:

■ *Marketing strategy* – the long-term setting of aims for the marketing function.

■ *Marketing planning* – the action plan for marketing activities.

■ *Marketing action* – the specific details to put the marketing plan into action.

The discussion you produce should clearly differentiate between the three areas if you are to achieve a high level in your writing.

The dangers of the four Ps

Above all other pieces of advice for tackling exam questions, we must end with a warning about the use and abuse of the marketing mix. There is a strong temptation to rely on the format of the marketing mix when answering any questions relating to the marketing section of the course. There will, of course, be times when this is appropriate. There are also times when it acts as a distraction from answering the actual question set in the examination.

The marketing mix is just one concept in the very broad area of marketing. There are other issues that are equally important, such as:

■ How do markets work?

■ How do consumrs behave?

■ How are decisions made?

■ What is the firm's product portfolio?

■ What is the firm's marketing strategy?

The best answers are those that can identify which of these aspects are central to the question being asked. A reliance on the single notion of the marketing mix will usually limit an answer.

Conclusion

Marketing is a fascinating area of the Business Studies syllabus. It has an enormous appeal because we see all sorts of interesting marketing activities going on around us – new products, new advertising campaigns and new ways of distributing products and services. However, student exam answers are very often descriptive and rather general. A good answer must consider how *a specific type of product* in *a specific situation* should be marketed, rather than any product. The marketing of a fork lift truck will be very different to the marketing of soft drinks. There is also a tendency in exam answers to focus on marketing *actions*, without sufficient thought given to the overall *objectives* and *strategy*. Ultimately, changing the packaging of a product will have limited effect on the firm's success if it is operating in the wrong market. Whenever you can, try to think whether the actual market conditions are appropriate for the firm (e.g. is the firm growing? Does a particular course of action fit with the firm's resources? Is the firm profitable?), as well as considering the detailed issues such as the price of the product. Good marketing answers take an integrated approach, both in terms of different aspects of the marketing (the pricing strategy must fit with the promotional strategy) and in terms of how marketing fits with the other functions of the business. Has the firm got the finance necessary to fund the proposed campaign? Can it manufacture on the scale required by an expansion into a new market segment? Does it have the sales staff required to achieve the objective of increasing market share? A good student never forgets the impact that marketing decisions can have on other aspects of a business and the need to co-ordinate a firm's plans to ensure the overall objective is fulfilled.

Good luck in your exams!

Appendix

Analysing marketing numbers

1 Elasticity of demand

a   Elasticity of demand measures the change in the level of demand in response to a change in another factor, such as price, income or advertising.

b   The general formula for calculating elasticity of demand is:

$$\frac{the\ percentage\ change\ in\ the\ quantity\ demanded}{the\ percentage\ change\ in\ another\ factor}$$

The specific formulae, therefore, are:

PRICE elasticity of demand =

$$\frac{the\ percentage\ change\ in\ the\ quantity\ demanded}{the\ percentage\ change\ in\ PRICE}$$

INCOME elasticity of demand =

$$\frac{the\ percentage\ change\ in\ the\ quantity\ demanded}{the\ percentage\ change\ in\ INCOME}$$

ADVERTISING elasticity of demand =

$$\frac{the\ percentage\ change\ in\ the\ quantity\ demanded}{the\ percentage\ change\ in\ ADVERTISING}$$

c   Analysing elasticities

   i   One of the most important reasons for calculating elasticities is for businesses to be able to see the effect of proposed changes. For example, price elasticity of demand will often be used to calculate the effect of a price change on the firm's total revenue.

   ii The effect on revenue can be summarised as follows:

	DEMAND IS PRICE ELASTIC	**DEMAND IS PRICE INELASTIC**
Price is increased	Revenue falls	Revenue rises
Price is decreased	Revenue rises	Revenue falls

iii Decisions ought not to be taken on the basis of elasticity of demand in isolation. Like all things in marketing, it must fit in with the overall marketing strategy and all the other marketing tactics being used. If the aim is market penetration, the firm may decide to reduce price even if the product is thought to be price inelastic. The fall in revenue may be acceptable to the firm in exchange for some increase in market share. However, given that the product is price inelastic, the firm may be better off looking for other, non-price measures to increase sales, such as advertising.

iv In reality, it is very difficult to know the exact level of elasticity for any product. There will be many different factors that have an effect on the level of demand. It is almost impossible to isolate a single factor and attribute a change to that one effect. Even using market research would not allow the level of elasticity to be determined with any great accuracy.

2 Forecasting

a All forecasts are based on assumptions. Check the assumptions made before making decisions on the basis of the forecasts.

b Long-term forecasts are usually more uncertain than short-term ones.

c Forecasts are often made on the basis of:

■ research data

■ extrapolation

■ correlation

i Research data is covered in detail in Chapter 4 of this book.

ii Extrapolation means taking existing trends and projecting them into the future. It assumes that the past is a good indicator of the future, which may be a flawed assumption. In addition, there may well be a difference between the short-term trend, that is what has happened in the past few months, and the long-term trend of the past years.

Often, there will be more than one extrapolation made from a given set of data. These will each have a different assumption, so that a range of results will be gained, from the most optimistic to the most pessimistic.

Extrapolation can give an indication of the future, but must be used in conjunction with all other available sources of information. Your sales may have gone up recently, but the economy was also in a boom phase. If the economy in now entering a recession, it is likely to be unwise to feel that your sales will continue climbing upwards.

iii Correlation is a way of finding a connection between the changes in two different variables.

It may find that as one variable rises, so does another. For example, it would be expected that a rise in the average temperature would be matched by a rise in the sale of ice creams. This is known as a positive correlation.

On the other hand, one variable may rise as another falls. Such a negative correlation would be expected between the price of rail tickets and the number of rail journeys made.

Finding a correlation, though, cannot be taken to mean that a change in one of the variables *causes* a change in the other – there will often be other factors at work at the same time. For example, BT may have found recently that its cutting the cost of calls for traditional land lines has been matched by a falling number of calls. This implies that if BT were to raise its prices, people would make more calls! Of course, the two factors have been influenced by a third, the growth of the use of mobile phones. Although the first two facts may be correlated, they have no direct causal relationship.

3 Sampling

a A sample is a representation of the whole population relevant to a decision. Firms need to use samples when it is too expensive or too time consuming for the firm to ask everyone questions.

b Firms need to:
    i Make sure the sample is as accurate a representation as possible.
    ii Be able to describe the key features of the sample (and so, by extension, the whole population).
    iii Know how reliable the sample findings are.

The sample can be made representative by:

■ avoiding bias in the selection of the sample

■ ensuring a large enough number of people are included in the sample

■ ensuring the data collection techniques are fair

■ ensuring the interpretation of results is done fairly

c The key features of the sample can be described by using **measures of central tendency** and **measures of dispersion**.

The measures of central tendency try to find the middle of the data. The main ones are the mean, median and mode:

■ Mean – this is the arithmetic average. Its value may not be reliable if it has been distorted by extreme values at one end of the data.

■ Mode – this is the figure that occurs most often. Its use is limited as it takes no account of any other reading or their scale.

■ Median – the middle of the range when placed in order. It takes no account of the magnitude of other readings.

Each of these measures has its limitations, but when taken together, they can help give some important features of the sample.

The measures of dispersion try to describe the spread of the data. The main ones are the range, the interquartile range and the standard deviation:

■ **Range** – gives the highest and lowest values in the sample. It can be distorted by extreme values.

■ **Interquartile range** – gives the values one quarter and three quarters of the way through the sample. It is more meaningful than the simple range.

■ **Standard deviation** – measures the average of all values away from the mean. It can be developed further to give meaningful data about the likelihood of events occurring.

Each of these, when taken together, can help form a clear picture of the extent of the sample findings.

4 Confidence levels

Since firms will almost always use samples, they can not be certain that the results they have achieved are true for the whole population. The standard deviation can be used to calculate the confidence level for a set of findings.

Most commonly, firms attempt to achieve a 95% confidence level, since:

a   such results ought to occur 19 times out of every 20, and
b   it is relatively easy to calculate.

The 95% confidence level is represented by the mean ±2 standard deviations. This is illustrated by the following example:

A sample survey finds that 65% of consumers would try the firm's new product. The firm, however, will only launch the product if it can be 95% certain that more than half of all consumers will try the product. Although the mean is 65%, and so above the 50% criteria, can the firm be sure that this applies to the whole population?

The firm has calculated the standard deviation as being 6%.
Therefore, two standard deviations for this data is (2×6) 12%.
The 95% confidence level, therefore, is the sample mean of 65% $\pm$ 12%.
The firm can be 95% certain that the true take up will be between $(65 - 12)$ 53% and $(65 + 12)$ 77%.
As far as the decision is concerned, the 50% criterion is bettered by the whole of the range for the confidence level, and so this firm will be able to launch its new product, being fairly certain that more than half of all consumers will try the product.

The decision, however, is only valid if:

■   the data has been collected and analysed without bias

■   the firm has used a representative sample for the whole population

Of course, there is still the possibility that this is the one time in twenty when the results do not apply. That is, however, the risk taken when using sampling.

Index